D1740742

COSTA BRAVA
COSTA DORADA

Authors:
Elke Homburg, Marion Golder

An Up-to-date travel guide
with 42 color photos
and 7 maps

NELLES

IMPRINT / LEGEND

Dear Reader: Being up-to-date is the main goal of the Nelles series. Our correspondents help keep us abreast of the latest developments in the travel scene, while our cartographers see to it that maps are also kept completely current. However, as the travel world is constantly changing, we cannot guarantee that all the information contained in our books is always valid. Should you come across a discrepancy, please contact us at: Nelles Verlag, Schleissheimer Str. 371 b, 80935 Munich, Germany, tel. (089) 3571940, fax (089) 35719430, e-mail: Nelles.Verlag@t-online.de

Note: Distances, measurements and temperatures used in this guide are metric. For conversion information, please see the *Guidelines* section of this book.

LEGEND

★★ ★★	Main Attraction *(on map)* *(in text)*	**Blanes**(Town) **Catedral** (Sight)	Places Highlighted in Yellow Appear in Text	⊖	National Border	
★ ★	Worth Seeing *(on map)* *(in text*	↙ ↙	Int'l, Nat'l Airport		Motorway	
					Expressway	
❽	Orientation Number in Text and on Map	**Prades** ·1201	Mountain (altitude in meters)		Principal highway	
					Main Road	
	Public or Significant Building	\ 13 /	Distance in Kilometers		Provincial Road	
		☀	Beach		Secondary Road	
	Hotel	🌳	National Park	⚓	Ferry	
	Market	🛈	Tourist Information	⑤⑤⑤	Luxury Hotel Category	
✝ ⛪	Church	∴	Ancient site	⑤⑤	Moderate Hotel Category	
⛫	Castle	∩	Cave	⑤	Budget Hotel Category *(for price information see "Accomodation" in Guidelines section)*	

COSTA BRAVA – Costa Dorada
© Nelles Verlag GmbH, 80935 München
All rights reserved

First Edition 2001
ISBN 3-88618-724-1 (Nelles Travel Pack)
ISBN 3-88618-769-1 (Nelles Pocket)
Printed in Slovenia

Publisher:	Günter Nelles	**Photo Editor:**	K. Bärmann-Thümmel
Editor-in-chief:	Berthold Schwarz	**Cartography:**	Nelles Verlag GmbH
Editor:	Beate Decker	**Color Separation:**	Priegnitz, München
English Edition Translator:	Kerstin Borch	**Printed by:**	Gorenjski Tisk

TABLE OF CONTENTS

LIST OF MAPS

CATALONIA

MAR

MEDITERRÁNEO

CATALONIA

0   15   30 km

Celtic-Iberian Period

700 B.C. The Iberian culture extends from southern Spain as far as present-day Catalonia. The Iberian settlement of Ullastret is founded. Celts enter the region from the Northeast; tribes mix and a Celtic-Iberian culture is founded.

Greco-Roman Period

circa 600 B.C. The Greeks establish their first center of trade at *Emporion* (Empúries) on the Costa Brava.

218-201 B.C. In the second Punic War the Romans defeat the Carthaginians who, in the meantime, conquered the Greek settlements. They then establish the province of *Hispania Citerior*, with *Tarraco* (Tarragona) as its main city. A comprehensive "Romanization" of the Iberian peninsula follows.

Visigoth Rule

414 A.D. The Visigoths invade Catalonia ("Gotalonia") and promote the Roman colony of *Julia Augusta Faventia Paterna Barcino* (Barcelona) to capital city.

From 587 onwards Christianity becomes the official religion of the Visigoth realm.

Moorish-Carolingian Rule

From 711 Arabs defeat Visigoth troops and in the following years conquer almost the entire Iberian peninsula, including Catalonia. The ensuing Christian re-conquering (*Reconquista*) first comes about in Northern Spain.

8th/9th centuries The Spanish Mark, introduced by the Carolingians, becomes the nucleus of the Catalan nation and therefore serves as a defense against the Moorish rule. Guifré el Pelós reunites several Catalan counties which are then taken under administrative rule in Barcelona.

985 Almansur, the Moorish Grand Vizier, conquers Barcelona but the city wins back its freedom in **988** without Carolingian help. Count Borell II then announces *Catalunya's* complete independence from Carolingian rule.

The Naval Power of Catalonia-Aragón

12th/13th centuries Catalonia and Aragón are united by a marriage. The new kingdom, with Barcelona as its capital city, becomes a strong maritime power. With the *Corts Catalans* - a corporative assembly of representatives of the aristocracy, clergy and middle classes - the first parliamentary government in Europe is established.

14th century Sicily, Naples and Sardina join the kingdom of Catalonia-Aragón, now one of the greatest trading powers in the Mediterranean.

Spanish Catalonia

1469 The marriage between Fernando of Aragón and Isabella of Castile results in the center of power

Moorish warriors (mural, 13th century, Museu d'Art de Catalunya in Barcelona).

being transferred to Castile. But the Catalans maintain a confident position and several revolts against the Spanish crown take place in the following centuries .

1492 The fall of Granada marks the end of an almost 800-year period of Moorish culture in Spain. The successful "Catholic monarchs" Ferdinand and Isabella excommunicate all Spanish Jews. In October Columbus reaches the coast of America, resulting in the focus of Spanish maritime trade being shifted from the Mediterranean to the Atlantic. Barcelona is officially excluded from any overseas trading and the fate and downfall of Catalonia is therefore sealed. Castilian Spain becomes a world power.

1516 200 years of Habsburg rule in Spain commence with Charles I. Under the reign of Philipp II Spain becomes "an empire in which the sun never sets".

1714 In the Spanish War of Succession Catalonia supports the Habsburgs. The victorious Bourbons

In 1936 international forces support the Republicans against Franco in Catalonia.

punish the Catalans for this by abolishing all of their national institutions and prohibiting the Catalan language.

1741 The first textile manufacturing company in Barcelona marks the beginning of Catalonia's progressive industrialization.

Mid-19th century Catalan nationalism grows with the upswing of the economy. The period of *Renaixença* marks a revival of Catalonia's independent history and culture.

1888 The great World Exhibition takes place in Barcelona, on the grounds of its former citadel. In the following years *modernism* - a Catalan version of Art Nouveau - develops and flourishes, particularly in Barcelona.

circa 1900 A wave of workers' revolutions shocks the city.

1929 Second World Exhibition in Barcelona, on Montjuic hill.

1931 Catalonia attains its first autonomy statute under the Republican government.

1936-1939 Spanish Civil War. On **26th January 1939** General Francisco Franco's troops enter the Republican stronghold of Barcelona. During the dictator's 36-year rule the Catalan culture and language are held in complete suppression.

Spain remains neutral in the Second World War.

After 1960 The age of mass tourism on the Costa Brava begins.

1975 After the death of Franco, Juan Carlos I de Bourbon becomes King of Spain and paves the way for the democratization of the country.

Self-government in Catalonia

1979 Catalonia receives its second statute of autonomy, which allows for a somewhat limited form of self-government. Catalan finally becomes one of the official languages of Spain.

1980 The conservative *Convergencia i Unio* (CiU) under Jordi Pujol wins the regional elections. To this day Pujol is president of the Catalan regional parliament, the *Generalitat.*

1986 EU membership for Spain. Barcelona is awarded the privilege of hosting the 1992 Summer Olympics. A complex re-development and extension of the city begins.

1988 Catalonia celebrates its 1000-year anniversary.

1989 Salvador Dalí, the great master of surrealism born in 1904 in Catalonia, is buried in his home town of Figueres on the Costa Brava.

1992 The XXV Summer Olympic Games are held in Barcelona and on the Costa Brava.

2000 Prime Minister José María Aznar and his People's Party PP (*Partitudo Popular*) win the absolute majority in parliamentary elections held in March and must no longer depend on the support of Jordi Pujol's CiU.

CATALONIA
Quintessential Mediterranean Landscape

Catalonia, located in northeastern Spain, is 32,000 square kilometers in area – about the same size as Belgium and is home to about six million people.

The vast geography of this region extends from the Pyrenees, whose highest peaks rise above 3000 meters in Catalonia, to the rocky **Costa Brava** in the north – that "wild" stretch of coastline between Portbou and Blanes, and further south to the flat "golden" **Costa Dorada**, which ends at the mighty Ebro delta. Between these lie the **Costa de Maresme** and **Costa del Garraf** – home to Barcelona's local beaches.

Further inland, holm oaks, cork oaks, forests of evergreen shrubs, almond and orange groves complete the picture of the archetypal Mediterranean landscape. And right in the middle of all this natural beauty lies **Barcelona**, the confident capital of Catalonia, which in the past few years has developed into one of Europe's most exciting metropolises.

Catalunya no es Espana

„Barça, Barça!" – when the battle cries of the F. C. Barcelona fans echo through the town and the *Ramblas* – the most famous strolling and posing boulevard in the city – is drowned in a sea of red and blue club flags, one will have realized that football means quite a lot to the Catalans. However, matches against archrivals Real Madrid tend to take on the character

Preceding pages: So much for overcrowding – there are still wonderfully quiet bathing spots just waiting to be discovered. Cadaqués – the famous artisan colony and truly the "most beautiful village in the world." Left: The Castilian Tower is not merely a popular acrobatic presentation, but it is also a symbol of Catalan unity.

of a genuine battle, merely coincidentally being fought on a football pitch, because all this hubbub is about more than just football! The roots of the age-old rivalry between the two mightiest Spanish cities, or in other words between Castilians and Catalans, can be explored if we dig a little deeper in the annals of history.

The decline of Catalonia as a maritime power began in the mid-15th century, when Isabella, Castilian heir to the throne, married Fernando of Catalonia-Aragòn, leading to the center of power being transferred inland. Columbus was still received in Barcelona in 1492 following his first voyage to America but subsequently this maritime nation was excluded from trading with the New World so that Seville would benefit in its place. With this drastic step Catalonia's decline into insignificance was sealed. What followed was the sad story of a nation losing its proud independence through unremitting suppression: under General Franco's dictatorship it was illegal to speak *Català* (Spanish: *Catalan)* in public. Being one of the Romance languages it bears more resemblance to the Provençal spoken beyond the Pyrenees rather than to *Castellano* or Castilian, i.e. Spanish.

Following the dictator's death rehabilitation finally got underway, supported in 1979 by King Juan Carlos' reinstatement of Catalonia's autonomy. Since then an independent parliament, the *Generalitat*, represents Catalan interests. In the meantime Catalan is once more one of the official languages of Spain, together with Castilian, Basque and Galician. The days of submission are finally over and there can no longer be any doubt: "Catalunya no es Espana" (Catalonia is not Spain).

No Pain, No Gain

In the same way that Catalonia was hailed the "Gateway to Europe" during Franco's dictatorship, the Catalans are

now building "gateways" or bridges between the mentalities of north and south. Efficiency in business and the ability to enjoy life go hand-in-hand here. A healthy balance between *Seny* – logic and human intellect, and *Rauxa* – enthusiasm and exuberance, determines Catalan life. After all, why should one not combine the pleasurable with the necessary? Business is best conducted over a good meal. As nationalistic and conservative as the Catalans might seem, they are equally open-minded and innovative. In any case, they are well armed for the 21st century – *Catalunya mes que mai* – Catalonia now more than ever !

Exploring the Costa Brava

For a long time it was mainly artists who surrendered to the inspiring "wild" beauty of these rugged coasts, blessed

Above: Business in full swing! Catalonia's beaches in summertime. Right: Gaudí's highly-individual style – the Casa Batlló.

with rocky bays and rich mediterranean vegetation, and it was they who became the forerunners of modern-day tourists. From the late 1950's onwards it was mostly Germans who hotly pursued their travel agents' promises of sunshine, sea and a southern way of life. The first hotel complexes quickly sprang up, quaint little fishing villages mutated into seaside resorts and fishermen transformed themselves into hotel and restaurant owners. Nobody cared to ask the dreaded question of just how much more tourism this coast could tolerate as long as the pesetas continued rolling in.

A holiday on the Costa Brava today? We are pre-programmed to instinctively picture mass resorts, loud discotheques, cheap fast food restaurants and sun worshippers squeezed together on beaches in sardine-like fashion. Costa Brava's cheap image caused tourist numbers to suddenly dwindle in the 1980's.

Without a doubt the clichés correspond to the reality of resorts such as Lloret de Mar or Platja d'Aro but, at the same time,

the "other" Costa Brava which successfully opposed the building boom and its sweeping consequences peacefully co-exists in direct proximity. So here and there tranquil bays have remained untouched and there are still destinations such as Cadaqués or Tossa de Mar into which tourism has entered inconspicuously and quietly found its place alongside the more traditional branches of business. And beyond the coasts there awaits an almost virginal hinterland, marking the beginnings of an entirely new regional identity. The nearby Balearic Island of Majorca initially set the tone a few years back when it shook off its cheap beer-guzzling image by promoting the natural beauty of its inland in a favorable light. Keeping this in mind it is now high time for a second, closer look at the coasts of Catalonia. So let's get going to the Costa Brava! Not forgetting the Costa Dorada, which also has much more to offer than mere sun, surf and sand.

He who rests, rusts

Of course water sports play a major role during the summer months! Tourists can expect majestic beaches and typically-warm Mediterranean waters (which can thankfully once again be allowed to boast their superior quality). Windsurfers continue to find their meccas along the northern Costa Brava and divers their dorados in Illes Medes.

Hiking, cycling and golf are sports mostly pursued inland and are all still relatively fresh items on the tourist menu. They certainly suit the new, sporty, active image that Catalonia has recently adopted.

Appreciation of Art and Culture

The Art Nouveau architect Antoni Gaudí, painters Salvador Dalí and Joan Miró, cellist Pau (Pablo) Casals and opera stars Montserrat Caballé and Josep (José) Carreras were or are all Catalan. There are almost as many art museums and music festivals – along the coasts and inland – as there are grains of sand on the beach. And you don't have to be a culture or archaeology expert to get the most out of it. Between Roman walls and medieval palaces, fantastic Art Nouveau creations and temples of modern design, there is a lot just waiting to be discovered. Works of art are seldom touched by the verdigris of centuries, rather they are presented in new and imaginative ways thanks to the Catalan talent for exposition.

A visit to Barcelona is a must for every holiday itinerary. The Catalan metropolis is appreciated by lovers of art and architecture, followers of fashion, gourmets, football and opera fans, those passionate about strolling and, above all, by lovers of life. After it was awarded the 1992 Olympic Games it underwent a tremendous facelift and sparkled to the heavens when Catalan opera diva Montserrat Caballé warbled off the Olympic anthem together with Freddy Mercury.

15

THE COSTA BRAVA

NORTHERN COSTA BRAVA
CADAQUÈS / FIGUERES
CENTRAL COSTA BRAVA
GIRONA AND SURROUNDINGS
SOUTHERN COSTA BRAVA
COSTA DE MARESME

Costa Brava

COSTA BRAVA

About a century ago Catalan writer Ferrán Agulló penned the name **Costa Brava**, which means "wild coast". With this name he perfectly characterized the rocky, rugged, windswept Mediterranean coastline of northern Spain, which stretches from Portbou near the French border as far as Blanes bordering with the province of Barcelona, and measures almost 200 kilometers in length.

At the end of the 19th century it was artists who discovered the unique quality of light, mild climate and rugged beauty of this coastline. Salvador Dalí, born in Figueres, lived and worked in Port Lligat by Cadaqués for a long time and many of his peers and admirers followed in his footsteps. By the 1930's the Costa Brava had become a destination for the intellectual avant-garde and, as is so often the case, it was these artists who paved the way to the Costa Brava for future tourists.

The increase in wealth due to the rebuilding of the economy after the Second World War attracted northern and mid-

Left: The Teatre-Museu Dalí in Figueres. Salvador Dalí was buried under an unadorned tombstone without any inscription in the former auditorium in which there is a huge surreal portrait of Gala.

Europeans to more southerly climes. Profit-seekers saw to it that cheap hotel complexes sprang up in no time and, in those days, not a single thought was spared for the consequences that mother nature and the countryside would have to suffer. The centers of mass tourism such as Platja d'Aro or Lloret de Mar, with their high-rise blocks and cheap entertainment quarters – bloating to resemble cities in the summertime but diminishing into ghost towns in the winter – nowadays make a chilling impression on the visitor. But thankfully the ruggedness of the region provided a physical barrier to its total building-up. Places like Cadaqués or Tossa de Mar have, despite the throngs of visitors, retained their original character, and when small, sandy, pine tree-lined bays appear between jagged rocks awash with the sparkling turquoise of the Mediterranean you realize that holiday dreams really can come true on the Costa Brava.

It isn't only sun-worshippers or water sports fanatics who get their money's worth on a Costa Bravan holiday. Hikers, cyclists and golfers come into their own in the region's interior and the necessary infrastructure to support this new trend has been established.

And some of the greatest European cultural history is at home here. Inland you'll find medieval churches, monaster-

ies and villages, but also shrines to some of the greatest art of the 20th century, which urgently await your pilgrimage. After the opening of the Teatre-Museu in Figueres in 1974 two further domiciles of Dalí were opened, the sum of which is now dubbed the "surrealistic triangle."

The coast becomes tamer beyond Blanes: the beaches stretch out and the frequent interruption of rocky outcroppings ceases. The Costa de Maresme, as this area of coastline is called, stretches all the way to the Catalan capital and it is these beaches the inhabitants of Barcelona call their own.

NORTHERN COSTA BRAVA
Portbou and Port de la Selva

The track width of Spanish trains is, apart from modern luxury coaches, traditionally different to that of Europe. That's

Above and right: Windsurfers' mecca Port de la Selva. In calm weather a hike to Sant Pere de Rodes makes for an interesting alternative.

why beyond the French border travelers must still listen carefully for the announcement "please change trains." For the 1929 World Exhibition in Barcelona the little border town of **Portbou ❶** was developed into the principle rail connection between France and Spain and it also received a magnificent new station. Considering the sheer dimensions of the tracks one would expect to find a large city beyond the station, not a modest town of 2,000 souls.

This small town, exuding the unmistakable flair indigenous to southern France, achieved tragic fame in September 1940. When Jewish author Walter Benjamin (1892-1940) fled to the U.S. via Spain and Portugal, he had to wait here for some papers necessary to continue his journey, but committed suicide here rather than surrender to the Gestapo.

His grave in the cemetery high above the town has always been well-visited and on the 50th anniversary of his death Jewish artist Dani Karavan created his much-acclaimed work entitled *Passages:*

Costa Brava

a passage of steps, which finally reveals itself as a dead-end, leads from the cemetery to the sea. With this piece of work the artist successfully depicts hopelessness from the viewpoint of the hunted.

From Portbou the coastal road winds past the small town of **Llança**, which lies about 1 kilometer inland, and further south to Port de la Selva. The small pebble bays which litter the coast here are sparsely visited, even in summer. The northern part of the "wild coast" is popular with natives and French day-trippers.

The prettiest, quietest and most peaceful town on this part of the coast is **Port de la Selva 2**. The modest north-facing beaches and strong winds of this fishing town, which could only ever cause raptures in fanatical windsurfers, ensure that it will always remain quiet and peaceful. It is pleasant to sit at one of the small harbor cafés in the afternoons, watch the fishermen bring in their catch and breathe in the salty sea air. On cooler days a very interesting hike is an attractive option: for the ruins of one of the most important me-

dieval Catalan monasteries, ***Sant Pere de Rodes 3**, visibly tower high above the town.

The oldest preserved part of this Benedictine monastery, which can also be reached comfortably by car, dates back to the 9th century. It achieved its considerable wealth through donations only and the extensive library made Sant Pere de Rodes one of the most important learning centers of the early Middle Ages. Decline set in here around the 14th century and the writings speak of its monks succumbing to a decadent and licentious lifestyle. When the last of the holy men left the monastery at the end of the 18th century all of its fine treasures had been stolen and lost forever.

The monastery complex, still a striking sight despite its dilapidation, has been undergoing restoration for a number of years. The monastery church is particularly impressive. It was built in the 10th/11th centuries and was the first major Romanesque building project in all of Catalonia. Measuring 37 meters in length and 15 meters in width it can certainly boast stately proportions. South of here the two-storied cloister connects to this church. The upper floor shows clear evidence of restoration but some columns with figure capitals still display the early artwork of medieval stonemasons.

A narrow path leads upwards from the monastery to the ruins of the fort of **San Salvador**. The magnificent view from these 670 meters, high above the coast, is well worth the exertion of the climb.

Artistic Center of *CADAQUÉS

Reaching ★**Cadaqués** ❹ marks your arrival at the famous, first-ever holiday resort on the Costa Brava. Its attraction isn't due to fine sandy beaches but rather to its unique flair. Even Dalí, who often spent summers on his parents' property here as a child, spoke highly of the quality of light and atmosphere of Cadaqués, and later had his home built in nearby Port Lligat. An entourage of writers and artists followed and set up their studios in the whitest and most beautiful village on the Costa Brava. The Bohemian atmosphere, in turn, attracted tourists, who to this day continue to be spellbound and enchanted by the ensemble of white houses in the midst of this stunningly beautiful bay. Angled cobblestone lanes with chic boutiques and original cafés make a simple stroll through this town feel like pure joy. The addition of high-rise developments and fast food restaurants was shunned from the very beginning, thanks to a concerned town council and Dalí's own concerted efforts. And so the tower of the baroque parish church **Parroquial Santa Maria,** with its much-treasured altar carved by Pau Costa, remains to this day the highest edifice in Cadaqués. The mainly younger visitors find this a worthwhile district for their nocturnal patrols in pursuit of entertainment. "To see and be seen" is the motto in the many restaurants and bars here.

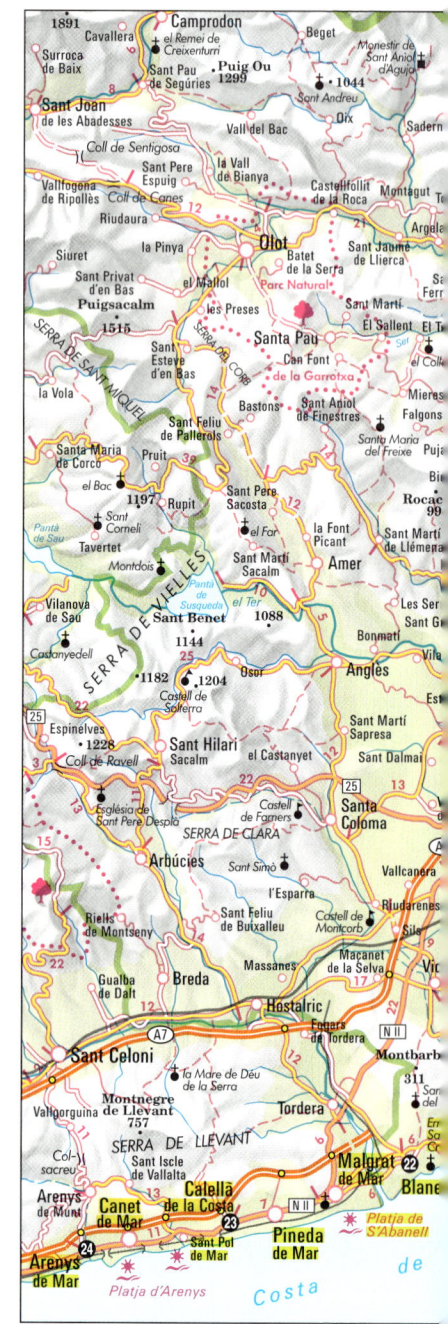

COSTA BRAVA

0   5   10 km

The fact that Cadaqués has remained an artists' town is evident from its many galleries exhibiting the works of both famous artists and the as yet unknown. The **Museu Perrot-Moore** in the town center ("dedicated to the talent and genius of the master Salvador Dalí") displays many sketches, watercolors and sculptures, including some lesser-known works from his youth. There are also paintings and drawings by Pablo Picasso on display. But the highlight of the exhibition is an old postal van dating from the 1930's in which Dalí, Gala, Miró and poet Garcia Lorca make their "surrealistic journey."

Dalí fans are obliged to make the pilgrimage to the *Casa-Museu Dalí in **Port Lligat**, only a 30 minute walk from Cadaqués, which already at a distance – thanks to its larger-than-life eggs – gives away its identity as surrealistic territory.

Above: Salvador Dalí once lived in the artists' sanctuary of Cadaqués. Right: The Golfo de Roses is lined with fine sandy beaches which stretch for many kilometers.

The artist and his muse, Gala, bought a whole row of fishermen's houses here, one by one, which were then connected together and converted into a bizarre residence which has been open since 1997. Beginning with the phallic swimming pool it lends an interesting insight into the complex mind of the great master.

**Cap de Creus

From Port Lligat the road continues to **Cap de Creus**, the easternmost tip of the Iberian Peninsula about 11 kilometers northeast of Cadaqués, where the Pyrenees appear to dissolve into the sea. This bizarre, lunar-like landscape sculpted by wind, weather and waves, has appeared in quite a few of the great master's paintings. According to Dalí, Cap de Creus is a place through which "a holy spirit drifts." Its spellbinding aura can be best appreciated from the viewing terrace of the lighthouse restaurant. The small bay between Cap de Creus and Cadaqués is ideal for snorkeling.

Costa Brava

From Roses to Figueres

The skyline of high-rise hotels provides advance warning that at **Roses** ❺ (12,000 inhabitants) you will have reached the largest tourist center in northern Costa Brava. But life beyond tourism is not extinct here: Roses has an important fishing harbor and, after Figueres, it is the most important trade center in this region.

The most significant monument in town is the huge **Citadel,** erected in the 16th century to protect the harbor. It encloses the remains of a Benedictine monastery and the 11th-century **Santa Maria** church. The ruins are evidence of this town's long history, founded in the 4th century by settlers from Rhodes. A 3-kilometer-long promenade skirts the main beach, **Platja Gran**, which boasts fine sand and a high water quality, and which in its south is bound by the **fishing harbor**. West and south of the town center are the urbanization projects of hotel and apartment complexes. Those wishing to flee the unsightly high-rise setting can reach the nearby beaches and bathing bays situated to the southeast and east of town. **Platja Canyelles Petites** and **Platja Canyelles Grosses** are several hundred meters in length, offer lots of swimming fun in glass-clear water, and have been thoughtfully developed. Hot tips for romantics are few and far between on the **Golfo de Roses** but it must be said that there are many beautiful bays such as **Cala Montjoi** or **Cala Jòncols**, situated 14 kilometers away.

Along the way to Figueres you'll touch upon the small town of **Castello d'Empúries** ❻ which experienced its heyday, as capital of the county of Empuries, in the Middle Ages. In its lanes time seems to stand still. By contrast the parish church of **Santa Maria**, which appears outsized when compared with the rest of the town, serves as a reminder of the glorious history of this place. It was built between the 13th and 15th centuries and, after the Cathedral of Girona, is the second largest church in the province.

Very expressive portrayals of the twelve apostles decorate the main portal and the beautiful figurine of Mary on the main altar is also well worth seeing.

When compared with the main town the seaside resort of **Empúriabrava** couldn't be more different, and was established in the 1960's as a completely new settlement. The canals running all the way through it allow for private moorings in front of the apartment houses and villas, which lend the town a fashionable appearance, which led it to become a popular destination with "weather refugees" from Europe, who bought their way in. This settlement is an absolute dream for every hobby skipper but fans of other water sports will also find a vast range of possibilities on offer on these fine, sandy beaches. The main beach, **Platja de Empúriabrava**, is wide and very well-maintained. However, Empúriabrava remains a foreign body in the Catalan coastal landscape and has always been something of an eyesore for environmental conservationists. The high water consumption of the many holiday apartments is actually threatening to drain the wetlands of Aiguamolls de l'Empordà (see p. 25) in the flat estuary of the Muga and Fluvià rivers.

Platja de Can Comes connects to the southern edge of the main beach and belongs to the National Park. It can be used by bathing guests, but not during the birds' breeding season, which lasts from 1st April until 15th June.

FIGUERES

Figueres ❼ is the trade and commercial center of the Empordà region and a lively town with about 32,000 inhabitants. The small plane tree-lined *Rambla*, as the Catalan streets meant for strolling

Right: The Torre Galatea of the theater-museum with its battlements of enormous eggs and spheres.

are usually called, is situated right in its center. During the day groups of pensioners meet up here and mothers with small children meet their peers. In the afternoon groups of schoolchildren join the crowd and everyone happily saunters about, in typical Catalan style with just a touch of southern French flair thrown in for good measure, far removed from the tourist bustle on the coast.

But this changes around the ****Teatre-Museu Dalí**, the legacy of the most famous son of the town and one of the most oft-visited culture sights in all of Spain. Salvador Dalí (see feature p. 76), born in Figueres in 1904, already caused a stir as a young man due to his very individual work. In the 1940's he achieved world fame and became a cult figure in the U.S. Yet the Catalan landscape remained his most important source of inspiration, beside his muse, Gala, who accompanied him from 1929 until her death in 1982. The couple lived in Port Lligat near Cadaqués (see p. 20) for many years. In the 1960's Dalí had already begun with plans for his own museum in Figueres' former town theater, which he gradually transformed into a veritable temple of his own art. Its doors were first opened to the public in 1974.

Stone loaves of bread decorate the walls, on which huge eggs perch, like battlements. In the inner courtyard of this fort of art Gala stylishly receives the guests in a black cadillac. The former theater auditorium is covered by a glass dome to which spiral ramps ascend over five floors. When faced with the breathtaking abundance of these imaginatively-presented exhibits visitors are inevitably drawn under the spell of the great master. The theater museum is much more than a gallery: it is a complete surrealistic work of art in its own right, with paintings, drawings and above all installations including the famous *Homage to Mae West*. A strange and sickly Dalí spent his final years following the death

of his beloved muse in nearby **Torre Galatea**. He finally found eternal peace in the crypt beneath the dome.

A worthwhile excursion leads from Figueres into the **L'Albera** region, which has belonged to Spain's most esteemed wine-growing regions for 25 years. Many of the wineries here are open for tastings. One place well worth visiting is the small L'Albera town of **Peralada**, situated 5 kilometers north of Figueres and dominated by a mighty fortress (14th to 19th century), providing an interesting setting for the casino here.

★Aiguamolls de l'Empordà

Thanks to the untiring dedication of conservationists the national park of ★**Aiguamolls de l'Empordà** was opened in 1983 and its 4,800-hectare expanse today surrounds Empúriabrava. A visitor center at the park entrance, which is accessible from the road leading to Sant Pere Pescador, offers plenty of informative material. Bird lovers in particular will get the most out of a hike through the park, along signposted trails. Amongst the rare species of birds at home here are crimson hens, herons and flamingos. But it is the innumerable stork nests which are the easiest to make out in springtime. The well-planned project of re-introducing the white stork here is showing its first positive results. With a little luck you may also see polecats and turtles.

Sant Pere Pescador

The further south you travel, the more gentle and tranquil the landscape becomes. The ever-dominant rocky bays of this region carry far gentler features and are surrounded by groves of pine trees and forests of holm and cork oaks. The beaches are wider here, with much finer sand, and they are generally more easily accessible.

The traditional fishing town of **Sant Pere Pescador** ❽ (*pescador* = fisherman) appears sleepy and reserved in comparison to the colorful lifestyle taking

place a mere 2 kilometers east, on the coast. But the beach here, measuring 6 kilometers in length, is highly-praised and it is mainly campers who laze around in its soft, light sand. Windsurfers from near and far appreciate the wind and waves.

And the tranquility of the national park inland remains well-protected, development projects continue to be refused and the **Platja de Sant Pere Pescador** remains a paradise for individualists.

L'Escala and **Empúries

L'Escala ❾ is famous for its *anxoves* (anchovies), a seafood specialty stored in salt and canned for export in various factories in the town. But they taste simply incomparable when served fresh at one of the bars in the old town. For some time now tourism has played a significant role in L'Escala. Holiday apartments, camp

Above: L'Escala and the Platja de Riells on the Golfo de Roses. Right: Empúries – evidence of Greek settlement in Catalonia.

sites and some hotel complexes either line the long and extremely well-kept main beach, **Platja de Riells**, which is bordered by **Port Pescadors** in the south, or are partially hidden in the nearby pine forests. A stroll northwards along the promenade connects L'Escala to more attractive beaches such as **Platja del Rec** but also to the ruins of **Empúries, considered one of the most important ancient archaeological sites in Spain and one of the most popular attractions in the region.

A natural harbor, long since buried beneath the sand, attracted Greek settlers here in the 6th century, who developed *Emporion* ("market place") into one of the most significant Greek trading centers in the western Mediterranean. In 218 B.C. the Romans invaded Spain and toward the end of the second century A.D. established a settlement for their veteran soldiers, connecting to the west of the Greek town. The Roman and Greek settlements were united as one during the reign of Caesar Augustus, under the name *Municipium Emporiae*. The decline of

this once-flourishing city set in around the second century, and it was not until the year 1908 that the previously destroyed and plundered Empúries saw the light of day once more, when excavations began.

The tour leads first through the remains of the Greek town. The foundations of private residences, temples, shops, the *agora*, the market place and other buildings have all been unearthed. The remains of an Early Christian basilica date back to the 4th century B.C., therefore, from the Late Roman period.

The excavated remains of the Roman town, which exceeded the proportions of its Greek counterpart considerably, stretch out behind the museum. Well-preserved mosaic floors were an integral part of the luxurious interior decoration of most of the villas at that time. At the forum, farther south, the main temple once rose up, the holy shrine of which was more than likely dedicated to Jupiter and Juno. The remains of a modest amphitheater lie outside the town walls.

The excavations are complemented by a **museum** displaying not only findings but also offering interesting information regarding the everyday lifestyles and religious cults of antiquity.

You can contemplate on your journey through history or simply let it fade out whilst relaxing beneath the shady pines of Empúries **beach**. If you would like to have your swimming fun at some of the other beautiful beaches in the region, then exit L'Escala in a southeasterly direction. Although the fine sand of **Cala Montgó** has long since been discovered by tourists it is still worth visiting, as this beautiful bathing bay is also ideal for hiking.

CENTRAL COSTA BRAVA
L'Estartit

The road from L'Escala leads further inland to the next large resort on the coast, L'Estartit. The small town of **Torroella de Montgrí** is well worth a stop along the way. And it is precisely this old town's unspectacular character that

makes it so special. Here, a mere 6 kilometers from the coast, the real and everyday lifestyle of Catalonia is lived. Stone houses line the streets. The townscape is characterized by the **Plaça de la Vila** with its beautiful arcade passages and medieval town hall, as well as the church of **St. Génis**, which dates back to the 15th century, at the northern edge of the old town.

The fortress of **Castell de Montgrí** is visible from afar and it has been watching over the town since the 13th century. Its lofty 300-meter-high position can be reached on foot after a one-hour walk, which is signposted and begins in the center of town. The splendid view over the plain and down to the sea is a reward worthy of the strains of getting there.

Although the earliest settlements were situated inland in order to protect them from pirate raids, the settlements of today

Above and right: Girona on the Riu Onyar possesses one of the most complete medieval town centers in all of Spain.

are all directly on the coast due to growing tourism and to satisfy the needs of water-loving tourists. And once upon a time **L'Estartit** was inhabited by only a few fishermen but today is one of the tourist meccas of central Costa Brava. Which comes as no surprise, as the **Platja Gran** is several kilometers long, wide and covered in fine, soft sand. It is lined with apartment complexes which quickly shot up and the tourist clientele here is mostly made up of young families with small children. The mostly modest hotels and guesthouses in the town center accommodate, above all, diving tourists, who have ideal diving territory at their disposal just off the coast around the ****Illes Medes**. This small chalk island, which towers steeply out of the water, once served as a military base. Since being placed under nature conservation twenty years ago only the largest island, **Meda Gran**, may be set foot upon. Diving and snorkeling trips, but also trips in glass-bottomed boats, can be booked in the town.

**GIRONA AND SURROUNDINGS

On a trip to Girona, the capital city of the eponymous province and the most important on the Costa Brava, you will see a unique medieval masterpiece, namely Girona's old town center which remains unparalleled in all of Spain. On the way there, you should make a detour to **Púbol**, where one of the corners of the famous "surrealistic triangle" is waiting to be explored, ★**Casa-Museu Castell Gala Dalí**.

Dalí bought a medieval castle in this sleepy little village in 1970, near highway C 255 and between La Bisbal and Girona. He had it restored and very individually decorated before presenting it to Gala as a present. Following redecoration, elephants with spiders' legs paraded through the garden and a golden throne stood waiting for the already-aged new lady of the house, who is said to have had her fair share of entertainment here with toy boys, whilst her husband was only received by her if a written invitation had been issued to him. To this day the garage contains the very cadillac in which Dalí, following Gala's death in 1982, had the remains of his idolized beloved transported from Port Lligat to Púbol. The master himself lived in this palace until 1984, but moved back to Figueres after being badly injured in a fire here.

Girona ⑩ is a university town with some 90,000 inhabitants and was founded in the 5th century by the Iberians. No less than four rivers flow through it: the Onyar, Güell, Galligants and Ter. Before it fell into the hands of the Counts of Barcelona in the 9th century Romans, Arabs and Franks had settled here due to its strategically advantageous location on a military road, the Via Augusta.

The Riu Onyar separates the bustling new town from the historic **old town.** The road leads from the Plaça Catalunya over the pedestrian Rambla de la Llibertad, with its many street cafés, and then uphill through narrow lanes to the Carrer de la Força in the former Jewish quarter **El Call**, where the significant but segregated minority – as was the case ev-

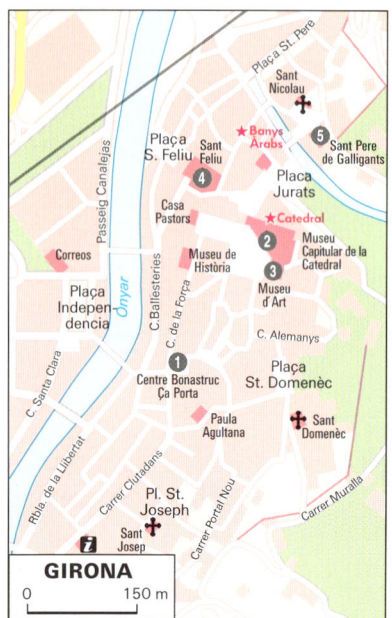

erywhere in Europe during that period – resided between the 9th and 15th centuries. The Jewish cultural center **Centre Banastruc Ça Porta** ❶ is situated on the Carrer de Sant Llorenç, once the site of a synagogue, where an exhibition on the history of *Sephardim* – as the Spanish-Portuguese Jews called themselves – in Girona is documented.

The imposing **★Cathedral** ❷, which sits on the highest point of the hill of the old town, can be reached via a set of majestic steps. Its building was already begun in 1312, but the early Gothic-style hall church wasn't finished until 400 years later. Despite the many years of building it radiates perfect harmony and is domed by the world's largest church vault – an extremely daring project in its time. The interior is unpretentious, all the

Above: The "Banys Àrabs" in Girona built in the Moorish style were not erected until the 13th century, 400 years after the expulsion of the Arabs. Right: Old stone houses are characteristic of Pals.

more so because of the diversity and splendour of the dome treasure in the **Museu Capitular de la Catedral** next door. The highlight of the collection is the **★★Tapiz de la Creacío**, an invaluable Romanesque tapestry 16 square meters in area, the detailed silk embroidery of which depicts scenes from the Creation. From the museum you reach the Romanesque cloisters which contain some extremely detailed, though largely weathered, figure capitals. The mostly religious works of art in the **Museu d'Art** ❸, situated in a former bishop's palace, are of a very high standard.

In the uniform cityscape there are two outstanding features, namely the parish church of **Sant Feliu** ❹ which was dedicated to St. Felix, patron saint of the town, containing several unusual Roman sarcophagi dating back to Pre and Early Christian times sunk into the walls, and the former Benedictine monastery of **Sant Pere de Galligants** ❺ (12th century). The latter today provides an atmospheric setting for the **Museu**

Arqueològic, which contains prehistoric findings, antiques and medieval exhibits. A collection of Jewish gravestones serves as a reminder that between the 9th century and 1492, before their excommunication by the infamous Catholic monarchs, one of the largest Jewish communities in all of Spain was at home here in Girona.

A particularly unique showpiece are the ★Banys Àrabs, the so-called Arab baths, which originated in the 12th century. Following their destruction one hundred years later they were restored back to their former glory. The fact that they date from Christian times is quite astonishing, considering that Christians in those days were "pure" in their religious beliefs but certainly not nearly as pure as their Islamic counterparts when it came to actual bodily cleansing. The elegant bathing rooms which resemble the traditional architectural arrangement of Roman thermal baths belong to the very few preserved Romanesque secular buildings in Spain today.

Iberian Settlement

Instead of taking the most direct route from L'Estartit to Begur via Pals you should really make plans for a detour including Ullastret and Peratallada.

The excavation site of ★Poblat Ibèric ⑪ near Ullastret provides evidence of one of the earliest settlements of the region. Mighty walls once surrounded the 6th-century B.C. Iberian settlement, which continued to exist until the early 2nd century A.D. Admittedly, you'll need to use a little inventiveness to imagine the former main street lined with residential houses and storerooms, and the hustle and bustle which took place here. The highest point in the settlement was the temple area, on which today a small museum stands. Here you'll find sketches, models and findings which will give you an idea of what everyday life was like for the Iberians. In fine weather, picnic tables are set up alongside each other around the site and the delicious smells emanating from the grills fill the air.

Medieval Treasures

Medieval flair is in the air in the towns of Peratallada and Pals. The narrow lanes in ***Peratallada ⑫**, behind huge stone walls (*Pedra Tallada* = chiseled stone), with their bumpy cobblestones, traditional restaurants – some with beautiful courtyards open in summertime, and a luxury hotel in the extended fortress **Castell de Peratallada**, all make for quite an atmosphere.

The town assemblage of ***Pals ⑬**, dominated by the church of **Sant Pere** and the **Torre de les Hores**, or clock tower, presents itself behind massive, perfectly-restored town walls. The antiquated narrow lanes appear almost too beautiful to still be inhabited. Houses here are made from golden-yellow sandstone, which appears to glow in the sunlight, and are decorated with flowers. In summertime this place is overrun with tourists from nearby resorts. It's best to visit Pals early in the mornings, or in the evenings when hotel guests taking half-board return back to their quarters.

Platja de Pals is the name of the settlement which developed along the coast, 5 kilometers from the main town. The beach, with its several kilometers of fine, soft sand, is capable of satisfying the needs of even the most spoilt bathing guests. Seeking out the town center though, will only lead you through a confusion of camp sites, apartment blocks and cheap stores. The effort will be fruitless. The surrounding area is developing more and more into a mecca for golfers, who have the choice of several courses here.

Begur

Begur ⑭ is the ultimate holiday destination for individualists. The jumble of

Right: Where would Catalan sparkling wine be without the cork oaks of Palafrugell?

nearby rock bays meant that there was never any room for the installation of mass tourism, so the holidayscape here shows both alternative and exclusive characteristics. The town attracts an international, mostly young crowd in the summertime, which appreciates the wide-ranging entertainment and many music bars. Despite this, there is no doubt that this town has retained its distinctly Catalan flavor.

The ruins of the 11th-century **Fort** on the hill, with its five battlement-defended towers, provide evidence that Begur used to be plagued by frequent pirate raids. From up here you can appreciate a panoramic view out over the plain and as far as the sea.

The town at the foot of the fort, with its confusion of narrow streets lined with boutiques and restaurants, exudes atmosphere. Building showpieces include the so-called **Casas Indianos**, built in the 19th century by Cuban immigrants who returned back to their home country in their old age as wealthy men.

If you are interested in the underwater life of the coast you'll find an informative exhibition, with several aquaria, in the nearby estate **Mas d'en Pinc**.

A well-developed road winds down the lush slopes from Begur to the small dreamy bays and beaches north and south of ***Cap de Begur** and past numerous exclusives residences. This is the quintessential Costa Brava.

Sa Riera, the longest sand bay in the Begur region, is relatively well but cautiously populated. Instead of the usual high-rise complexes, small hotels and guesthouses attract individual travelers for whom the atmosphere is far more important than the quality of perfectly-fashioned touristic infrastructure. If the beautiful, but in summertime popular, bathing bay becomes a little too busy for your liking, you can hike further in a northerly direction to the nudist beach of **Platja de la Illja Roja.**

Costa Brava

The rocky bays of **Aiguafreda** and **Sa Tuna** are strewn with stones and pebbles and are only partially suitable for swimming. To make up for this, there's a nice little harbor to see in Aiguafreda.

Leaving Begur in a southerly direction you'll come to a fork in the road, the turn-offs of which lead to Fornells and Aiguablava. The main road leads on to Tamariú and Calella de Palafrugell.

Platja de Fornells is only open to tourists in a few spots. There's a little harbor and an exclusive beach belonging to the **Hotel Aiguablava**, which is one of the top-class establishments on the Costa Brava. The villas stuck to indentations in the cliffs outline the classy atmosphere of this bay. The neighboring bay of **Aiguablava** is no different. The beauty of the eponymous beach, **Platja de Aiguablava,** with the austere luxury hotel **Parador Nacional Aiguablava** towering in the background, is no secret anymore and as it's only about 100 meters in length the towels do tend to be lined up side-by-side in summertime.

Palafrugell

Palafrugell ⑮, south of Begur, is the largest town in central Costa Brava with about 20,000 inhabitants. Cork production dominated trade here for almost 200 years before tourism conquered the area and promoted itself to the primary source of business. Cork reserves in the nearby cork forests are manufactured mainly into bottle corks. A veritable boom set in when Catalan wine growing expanded in Penedès following the 19th-century birth of *Cava*, a Catalan sparkling wine. Palafrugell is still the most important cork manufacturing location in Catalonia today and this is well-documented in an interesting exhibition at the **Museu del Suro**.

The most famous son of the town, Catalan journalist and writer Josep Pla (1897-1981), dealt in his work mainly with the cultural traditions of the Costa Brava. In the house of his birth a cultural institute, **Fundació Josep Pla**, was established.

The coast's most stunning beaches were quickly monopolized by the tourists of the 20th century, but they nevertheless remained peacefully serene. This patch of coast is not the territory of package-tourists but above all of Catalans who spend their weekends in their summer houses here.

By contrast, the three bays before Palafrugell, in **Tamariú,** are a lot more laid-back. In winter, Tamariú turns back into a fishing village with around 100 inhabitants and many small boats, which lend the bay occasional dots of colour. In summer, visitors are most definitely in the majority, but thankfully the rocks prevent major growth meaning that, also in the future, Tamariú will remain a holiday town in which small children will never get lost. The local beach, **Platja de Tamariú**, is flat and suitable for small children.

Above: The pretty resort of Callela de Palafrugell. Right: Cova d'en Daina – the dolmens of Romanyà de la Selva.

Those for whom Tamariú is just a little too quiet will find that **Llafranc** has more to offer. A harbor and recently a luxury hotel above the town attract a different crowd of visitors. The coarse-grained sand beach of **Platja de Llafranc**, 300 meters in length, runs alongside the promenade.

Calella de Palafrugell, connected with Palafrugell by highway and with Llafranc by footpath, is a livelier place with even more to offer. Several small beaches, all of them well-maintained but not necessarily with fine-grained sand, are located next to each other. Friendly little hotels, guesthouses and restaurants are scattered throughout the old town. Holiday resorts lie discreetly inland.

Something you simply must try once in Calella de Palafrugell, if you get the chance, is a specialty called *Cremat*: coffee flambéed with rum.

The cultural highlight of the year, the *Cantada d'Havaneres,* takes place on the first Saturday in July. This song festival is reminiscent of and holds in remembrance

the wistful song of passengers to Cuba, accompanied by guitars and accordions.

In **Cap Roig,** south of Calella, the ★**Jardí Botànic** (Botanical Garden), established by a colonel of Russian descent and his English wife in 1927, is well worth visiting. The Mediterranean flora will spellbind you in olfactory seduction and visual beauty, and you will repeatedly catch stunning panoramic views out over the coast.

SOUTHERN COSTA BRAVA

In southern Costa Brava the coastline peters out and becomes flatter, bays cutting deep into the rocks become scarcer, while long beaches benefit large-scale development for mass tourism, which has already disfigured several towns beyond recognition. Towns like Tossa de Mar decided early on for a cautious approach. The stark contrasts between the sins of tourism and natural beauty are far more noticeable here than in the northern part of Costa Brava.

Between Palamós and Blanes

The central focal point of **Palamós ⓰**, dating from the 13th century, was always the harbor. In the Middle Ages fleets destined for conquests set out from here and in 1571 the Spanish armada, under the command of Juan d'Austria, left this harbor to defeat the Turks in the naval battle of Lepanto.

The harbor awoke to new life with the development of the cork industry and today Palamos is the most important harbor for exporting cork. But the fishing industry also played its part in tourism having been halted on its path of becoming the main industry here.

A cape divides the town into two halves. The fishing harbor and behind it the old town, which actually developed from a fishing settlement, are situated on the southern side. The leisure harbor is situated on the northern side of the cape. The modern business development which lies behind it is anonymous in appearance. South of the fishing harbor the **Platja Gran de Palamós** begins, flanked by the promenade. Behind it the tourist town of Palamós with its obvious lack of original or imaginative architecture sprawls out. And although the high-rise backdrop is not exactly a feast for the eyes, the wide sandy beach is genuinely very attractive and the colorful range of restaurants and bars in the old town is most inspiring. And for those tourists who appreciate the bubbly atmosphere of a town not solely catering to the needs of tourists will certainly have an enjoyable holiday here. A worthwhile alternative to the sand beach is the bay of **Cala de la Fosca** northeast of the center and conveniently accessible by public transportation.

A trip into the beautiful hinterland of the **Serra de les Gavarres** will lead you via **Calonge** to **Romanyà de la Selva ⑰** and simultaneously back in time – into early Spanish history. A road forks off to **Cova d'en Daina** shortly before reaching the small town with its many attractive restaurants. Amid this pastoral landscape a cult site with dolmens and megalithic stone circles was founded around 4,000 years ago. Closeby, early historic monuments in the middle of the cork oak forests provide an ideal setting for a country picnic.

The small town of **Sant Antoni de Calonge** has almost grown together with Palamós. The beach of Palamós is continued here, with its not so fine-grained **Platja de Sant Antoni** and the **Platja de Torre Valentina.**

The road to Sant Feliu leads further along the coast. But there is also an additional coastal road *(Cami de Ronda)* which bypasses a whole range of sandy bays, which are partly open to the public during high season, offering the usual array of amenities.

Right: A gem along the Costa Brava – the lovingly-restored "Vila Vella" in Tossa de Mar on the Platja Gran.

The pine groves which once lined the **Platja Gran** have long since been felled. The skyline of skyscrapers in **Platja d'Aro ⑱** has, by contrast, expanded with unstoppable speed in the past decades. The population of this resort hovers around the 100,000 mark during the summer months. Tourists seeking action and variety, perfect touristic infrastructure and unlimited swimming fun on long sandy beaches, will have come to the right place.

Connected to the northern end of the coarse-grained main beach, which stretches for several kilometers, and behind a rocky outcrop, is the bay of **Cala Rovira**. It is the first of several more bays of its kind, which positively line the aforementioned coastal road from Palamós (⑯).

Particularly families with small children will enjoy the aquatic amusement park, **Aquadiver**, just off the bypass road.

The former main town inland, **Castell d'Aro**, today only holds significance as a day trip destination. Beside the **Castell de Bendormiens**, which has suffered many destructions since the 11th century, you'll find a doll museum, **Museu de la Nina**, which holds over 350 exhibits and is a worthwhile trip for not only younger doll fanatics.

In Platja d'Aro things revolve around the requirements of the tourist masses, but in contrast to this the "higher society" members of the suburb of **S'Agaró** prefers to congregate amongst themselves. Already in the 1930's the wealthy Catalans built their summer homes here. The **Hostal de la Gavina** is the oldest luxury hotel on the coast and has so far accommodated all the big names, Hollywood stars and royalty alike.

If you're looking for relaxation during your holiday rather than action in nightclubs and discotheques you'll do best in **Sant Feliu de Guíxols ⑲** south of here. After experiencing the satellite town of Platja d'Aro it will surely be soothing to

Costa Brava

stroll and browse through the old town of Sant Feliu.

The Plaça de Monestir, with its ruins of the **Sant Feliu** Benedictine monastery which dates from the time of Charlemagne, provides evidence for the once-rich history of this place. The name of the town derives from the monastery dedicated to St. Felix, who suffered martyrdom not far from here in 304. The promenade of **Passeig de Mar** which dates from 1834, lined with several villas in the *modernistic* style of Catalan Art Nouveau, gives the impression of an elegant seaside resort. Dignified representatives of the "good old days" include the **Casino dels Nois**, which helped revive Moorish stylistic elements toward the end of the 19th century, or the **Casa Patxot** (house number 40), the seat of the trade board. A short walk leads from the promenade to the **Plaça del Mercat** (market place) with its town hall and stylish market hall, in which most of the action takes place before noon. **Platja de Sant Feliu**, the local beach, is more suitable for stroll-

ing than swimming, but north of the town center a lovely bay provides excellent swimming, namely **Platja de Sant Pol**.

On the hill of Sant Feliu, the **Puig Castellar** crowned by the modest **Ermita de Sant Elm**, the writer Ferran Agulló is said to have once stood and penned the expression *Costa Brava* (wild coast). The view remains, to this day, inspiring.

A drive along the ****coastal road**, which winds it way for 22 kilometers from Sant Feliu de Guíxols to Tossa de Mar, belongs to the highlights of any Costa Brava trip. Grandiose views of the rocky coasts being hammered by the thundering sea repeatedly appear. The most beautiful bays remain free of people even in high season as they're only accessible from the sea. But the popular **Platja del Senyor Ramon** can easily be reached without any problems and a turn-off after 35 kilometers will lead you to it.

*Tossa de Mar ⑳ which was founded by the Romans is one of the true pearls of the Costa Brava and one of the places with the longest history of tourism. Like

Cadaqués, Tossa was the seat of a colony of artists in the 1920's. Even Marc Chagall spent several months in the "blue paradise" of Tossa.

The medieval *vila vella* (old town), fortified with walls and towers in its homogenous architectural style, was declared a protected historical site early on thanks to the foresight and care of the town administration. Yet it doesn't at all give the impression of being an open-air museum: it is actually still inhabited. In the midst of the confusion of lanes lies the former governor's palace, which today houses the **Museu Municipal**. Exhibits from the nearby Roman excavation site bring to one's attention the glorious history of Tossa as an artistic colony, not to mention the collection of paintings including several works by Chagall. Innumerable bars and terrace cafés invite you to fully appreciate the wonderful atmosphere whilst enjoying a *copa*.

From the **Lighthouse** perched on the highest point of the old town you can look down onto the wide **Platja Gran**, the northern end of which is connected to the equally attractive **Platja Mar Menuda**. South of the town center, the small bay of **Platja d'Es Codolar** is beautiful, but relatively difficult to reach.

History enthusiasts will be interested to know that in the **Vila Romana** on Avinguda del Pelegrí, north of the business quarter, they are actually following the tracks of a small Roman settlement dating from the 1st to 5th centuries.

Upon entering **Lloret de Mar** ㉑ it's hard to believe that the history of this town dates back over 2,000 years. Discotheques and fast food restaurants completely dominate this small town, which 50 years ago still slumbered as a peaceful little fishing village. Quite unlike Tossa, the development of this town continued unbounded. Today, Lloret often has to take the rap as the perfect example of

Above: Lloret de Mar is especially popular with younger tourists. Right: Strolling around the vegetable market in Blanes – a welcome alternative to the monotony of the beach.

malformation through mass tourism, but at least the town council appears to have learned from its past mistakes: the development of new holiday accommodation is no longer permitted. And the popularity of this bustling seaside resort remains unaffected by any negative propaganda. The mostly young clientele find their amenities and entertainment round the clock, usually at very low prices.

The main beach, **Platja de Lloret,** is accordingly overcrowded, but extremely well-equipped. Everything is available here in abundance, whether catering, refreshments or sports possibilities. The only way to escape is by fleeing westward to the connecting **Platja de Fenals**.

The **Ermita Santa Cristina**, located between Lloret de Mar und Blanes, is home to an annual festival every 24th July. The *festa major* is the celebration of its patron saint, St. Cristina. According to legend her remains were thrown into the sea in the year 300, close to the Italian town of Bolsena. After a long time the body drifted ashore, completely un-

scathed, at Lloret and was retrieved by fishermen. The miracle is honored by means of a sea procession organized by local fishermen and a subsequent traditional meal of stew.

The stunning sandy bay of **Platja de Santa Christina** lies at the foot of the small church.

Blanes ㉒, the southernmost town on the Costa Brava at the estuary of the Río Tordera, is simultaneously the largest settlement on the coast with 26,000 inhabitants. Nevertheless, in comparison to its neighbor Lloret de Mar, it appears almost cosily intimate. The reason for this is surely that Blanes has two successful and dependable industries of its own, textiles and fishing, and is not solely dependent upon tourism. Therefore the number of hotels here, in comparison with the smaller town of Lloret, appears almost modest. Most vacationers stay in the spaciously-designed camp site outside the town center. In contrast to other towns surviving solely from the travel industry, Blanes is by no means a ghost town in

winter. The **fishing harbor** at the eastern edge of local beach is one of the largest on the Costa Brava. The subsequent auctioning of daily catches brought in by the fishermen is a welcome alternative to the usual routine the seaside tourists are accustomed to. The auction hall itself is not open to tourists, but the bar on the first floor allows a peek inside. If you want to sample some freshly-caught fish, you'll be spoilt for choice in the restaurants along the harbor.

The center of attraction in the inner city is the beautifully-finished **Font Gòtica**, a 15th-century fountain bearing the coat of arms of the mighty Counts of Cabrera, who influenced the history of Blanes between the 11th and 17th centuries. Not far from here, to the north, stands the 14th-century parish church of **Santa Maria**. It once formed part of a complex of buildings connecting to the Cabrera palace.

Above: In the botanical gardens of Blanes. Right: Terrace café on the beach of Callela de la Costa.

The town, which was already renowned in Roman times under the name of *Blanda*, expands out beneath the 166-meter-high mountain of **Sant Joan,** bearing a chapel of the same name, and the **Castell de Sant Joan** dating all the way back to the 11th century. All that remains of the Castell de Sant Joan is the tower, which dates back to the time of Charles V. In the botanical gardens on the fortress slopes, **★Jardí Botànic Mar i Murtra**, no less than 4,000 species of plants from five continents are being cultivated. During the relaxing stroll through the glorious Mediterranean fauna with views of the deep-blue sea you simultaneously get a graphic lesson in botany.

Although the local beach, the **Platja de Blanes**, is coarse-grained and not very attractive, the wide **Platja de S'Abanell** bordering on its south with its 2.5 kilometers in length, is more so. It is big enough for water sports such as surfing or sailing.

In **Marineland Costa Brava,** between Blanes and Malgrat de Mar, families are guaranteed an exciting day because this

aquatic park offers more than its counterparts. As well as the usual swimming pools, water slides and playgrounds there are several shows daily featuring sea lions, dolphins and parrots.

COSTA DE MARESME

The border between the provinces of Girona and Barcelona lies south of Blanes. The Costa Brava merges into the **Costa de Maresme**, which up until a few years ago was still part of the Costa Dorada. The beaches of Maresme are several kilometers long, but narrow and loud because from Malgret de Mar onwards all the towns blend into one another without apparent boundaries due to the presence of highway N II leading from Malgret toward Barcelona and also because of the railway line Girona-Barcelona.

One can easily imagine that swimming amidst the stench of the emissions of innumerable cars, which are regularly immobilized in weekend traffic jams, to be quite an unpleasant experience; particu-larly as the already narrow beaches, which can only be reached via underpasses, have to be shared with all the daytrippers from Barcelona. Yet the towns on the Costa de Maresme benefit from their well-developed tourist infrastructure and the low prices of their simple and sometimes anonymous accommodations, which in turn provides a high density of visitors in **Malgrat de Mar, Pineda de Mar** or **Canet de Mar**.

Calella de la Costa ㉓ is also known as *Calella de los Alemanes,* a clear indication of this resort's main clientele.

Two resorts, however, boast very individual traits in comparison with the apparently interchangeable resort settlements on the Costa de Maresme: one of these gems is the pretty old town of **Sant Pol de Mar**, situated on a hill, and the other is **Arenys de Mar** ㉔ with its medieval lanes and fishing and yacht harbors. The **Museu Marès de la Punta** brings to our attention the old handicraft traditions of old such as the art of lacemaking, which was once so popular in this region.

BEGUR

Patronat de Turisme, Pl. Esglesia 8, tel. 972 624020, fax 972 623588.

Aiguablava, Pl. de Fornells, tel. 972 622058, fax 972 622112, top-class hotel on a small rocky bay. **Parador de Aiguablava**, Pl. d'Aiguablava, tel. 972 622162, fax 972 622166, superb location.

Sa Riera, Pl. de Sa Riera, tel. 972 623000, fax 972 623460, friendly hotel with great views over eponymous bay.

Rosa, C/ Forgas y Puig 6, tel. 972 623015, family-run hotel in the middle of Begur's old town.

Can Torrades, Concepció Pi Tató 5, tel. 972 622881, delicious grilled dishes (also vegetarian) in a rustic setting. **La Pizzeta**, C/ Ventura Sabater 2, tel. 972 623284. Pizzas and other dishes in a lively garden-restaurant.

Havanna, Concepció Pi Tató 3, music bar.

BLANES

Patronat Municipal de Turisme, Pl. de Catalunya s/n, tel. 972 330348, fax 972 334686.

Patacano, Passeig Cortils i Vieta 12, tel. 972 330002, traditional restaurant on beach promenade with wide-ranging fish dishes.

Jardí Botànic Mar i Murtra, Apr-Oct: 9 am-6 pm daily; Nov-Mar: Mon-Fri 10 am-5 pm, Sun 10 am-2 pm. **Marineland**, open from Easter-Oct: 10 am til sundown, daily, situated along the road between Palafolls and Malgrat.

Fish Auction daily at the harbor, 4-7 pm.

CADAQUÉS

Oficina d'Information Turistica, C/ des Cotxe 2, tel. 972 258315, fax 972 159442

Playa Sol, Pl. Pianc 5, tel. 972 258100, fax 972 258054, top-class hotel with pool and tennis courts, closed Jan/Feb.

La Residencia, Av. Caritat Serinyana 1, tel. 972 258312, fax 972 258013. An original, right in the center of town. Lovers of artistic flair will not notice the dust of the last few years. **Blaumar**, C/ Massa d'Or 21, tel. 972 159020, fax 972 159336. Small hotel, very good value for money. Small garden, swimming pool and lots of peace and quiet on the edge of town.

La Galiota, Carrer Narcís Monturiol/ Riba Nemesio Llorens 9. tel. 972 258187. Speciality restaurant which has earned Michelin stars. **Casa Anita**, C/ Miquel Rosset 1, tel. 972 258471, home cooking in a relaxed and sociable atmosphere.

L'Hostal, Passeig 8, legendary trend spot with dance floor. Dalí was a regular and Mick Jagger has also been spotted here. **La Habana**, Punta d'en Pampa. Comfortable bar for romantic souls.

Museu Perrot-Moore, Carrer Unió/Riera de Sant Vicente, June-Sept: Mon-Sat 10:30 am-1:30 pm and 4-8 pm, guided tours at 5 pm and 6:30 pm. **Casa-Museu Salvador Dalí**, in the Port Lligat part of town, mid-June to mid-Sept: Tue-Sun 10:30 am-9 pm, otherwise Tue-Sun 10:30 am-6 pm, closed Nov to mid-March. As the tour can only be made with a guide one should pre-book by telephone, tel. 972 258063.

CALELLA DE PALAFRUGELL

Oficina de Turisme, C/ de les Voltes 9, tel. 972 614475.

Sant Roc, Pl. de l'Atlàntic 2, tel. 972 6114250, fax 972 614068, relaxed hotel with garden and glorious view out over the bay and town. Steps down to the beach.

Plankton, C/ de Codina 16, tel. 972 615081. Small and inexpensive guesthouse.

El Didal, Pl. del Port Bou, good fish dishes, at the harbor.

La Bella Lola, Pl. St. Pere 4, rustic bar for fans of melancholy Havaneres singing, snacks available.

Jardí Botànic de Caixa de Girona, Cap Roig, in summer from 9 am-7:30 pm daily. In winter until 6 pm.

Diving Center Poseidon Nemrod Club, Pl. Port Pelegri, tel. 972 615345.

EMPÚRIABRAVA / CASTELLÓ D'EMPÚRIES

Oficina de Turisme, Puigmal 1, Empúriabrava, tel. 972 450088.

Oficina de Turisme, Pl. dels Homes 1, Castelló d'Empúries, tel. 972 156233.

Briaxis, Port Principal 25A-30C, tel. 972 451545, fax 972 451889, apartment complex with its own jetties.

Allioli, Castelló Nou, tel. 972 250320, fax 972 250300, rustic rooms in an old estate near Castelló d' Empúries.

Canet, Pl. Joc de la Pilota 2, tel./fax 972 250340, newly-renovated house with pool, in the center of Castelló d' Empúries.

El Portal de la Gallarda, C/ Pere Stany 14, nice nighttime haunt, with terrace.

Parc Natural Aiguamolls de l'Empordà, Info center El Cortalet, 9 am-2 pm and 4-7 pm daily, tel. 972 454222, access via the road to Sant Pere Pescador.

BOAT TOURS: **Canaltour**, Sector Alberes 233, tel. 972 452579, round-trips through the canals. **Eco Boats Electric**, Poblat típic s/n, tel. 972 454946, rental of electric boats for driving oneself.

FIGUERES

Oficina de Turisme, Pl. del Sol. tel. 972 503155, fax 972 673166.

Durán, C/ Lasacua 5, tel. 972 501250, fax 972 502609, traditional and charming hotel, even Dalí appreciated the no-nonsense cuisine in its restaurant.

Teatre-Museu Dalí, Pl. Gala-Salvador Dalí, Oct-June: Tue-Sun 11:30 am-5 pm, July-Sept Tue-Sun 9 am-8 pm. **Museu de l'Empordà**, Rambla 2, regional museum with paintings by contemporary Catalan painters. July-Sept: Tue-Sun 11 am-1 pm and 3:30-7 pm, Oct-June 11:30 am-5:15 pm.

GIRONA

Oficina de Turisme, Rambla de la Llibertat 1, tel. 972 226575, fax 972 226612

Carlemany, Pl. Miquel Santaló, tel. 972 211212, fax 972 214994. Best hotel in town, on the edge of the town center.

Bellmirall, C/ Bellmirall 3, tel. 972 204009, romantic guest house with a very informal atmosphere, in the middle of the old town.

Peninsular, C/ Nou 3, tel. 972 203800, fax 972 210492, simple hotel near the old town.

YOUTH HOSTELS: **Alberg de Joventut**, C/ dels Ciutadans 9, tel. 972 218003, in a beautiful old town house.

Albereda, C/ Albereda 7, tel. 972 226002, excellent Catalan cuisine, wonderful ambience, closed Sundays. **Cal Ros,** Cort Reial 9, tel. 972 217379, popular family restaurant. **Le Bistrot**, Pujada Sant Domènec 4, charming coffee house in the old town with a small variety of warm dishes. **Selva Mar**, C/ Santa Eugánia 81, tel. 972 236329, delicious fish dishes and crustaceans.

In summertime the student youth congregates in the **open-air bars** in the Parque de la Devesa.

La Catedral, Tue-Sat 10 am-2 pm and 4-7 pm, Sun 10 am-2 pm. **Museu Capitular,** Tue-Sat 10 am-1 pm and 4:30-7 pm, Sun 10 am-1 pm. **Museu d'Art**, Pl. dels Apòstols, Tue-Sat 10 am-6 pm, Sun 10 am-2 pm. **Els Banys Arabs**, C/ Rei Ferran el Catòlic, April-Sept: Tue-Sat 10 am-7 pm, Sun 10 am-2 pm, Oct-March: Tue-Sun 10 am-2 pm. **Museu Arqueològic**, in the Romanesque Benedictine monastery of **Sant Pere de Galligants**, C/ Santa Llúcia 1, Tue-Sat 10 am-1 pm and 4:30-7 pm, Sun and holidays 10 am-1 pm.

L'ESCALA

Oficina de Turisme, Pl. de les Escoles 1, tel. 972 770603.

Nieves Mar, Passeig Maritim 8, tel. 972 770300, fax 972 773605, pleasant accommodation for sports fans, on the beach promenade.

El Roser, C/ Església s/n. tel. 972 770219, fax 972 774529, friendly guest house in the old town.

Ampurias, Afores, tel. 972 770207, simple, but its location on the bay – a stone's throw from the ruins, couldn't be more perfect.

YOUTH HOSTELS: **Alberg de Joventut Empúries**, Les Coves 41, tel. 972 771200.

El Paradís, Av. Montgó 260, tel. 972 770200, 100 meters from the beach, shady, with tennis courts, pool and childrens' playground.

Els Pescadors, Port d'en Perris 5, tel. 972 770 728, fresh fish at reasonable prices. **La Taverna del Sal**, C/ Santa Maxima 7, simple, inexpensive, good.

Ruines d'Empúries, Oct-May: 10 am-6 pm daily, June-Sept 10 am-8 pm daily, 2 kilometers north of L'Escala.

L'ESTARTIT

Oficina de Turisme, Passeig Maritim 47, tel. 972 758910, fax 972 757619.

Miramar, Av. de Roma 7, tel. 972 758628, fax 972 757500, small, unpretentious hotel with lovely shady garden and pool.

Les Illes, C/ Illes 55, tel. 972 758239, fax 972 750086, simple, basic hotel, rooms partly with harbor view, connected to a diving base. **Santa Clara**, Passeig Maritim 18, tel. 972 751767, fax 972 751149, informal and friendly guest house, some of the rooms with sea views.

Les Salines, Passeig Molinet 5, tel. 972 758773, here one can really binge on the superb seafood on offer, higher prices. **Els Valencians,** C/ de Montgó 29, for fans of *paella Valencia*. **Casi Casi**, Passeig Maritim 22, smart tapas bar. **Termar**, C/ Santa Anna, locals like to eat here. Popular, inexpensive rice dishes include *arròs negre* ("black rice" – with sepia).

Mariscal, C/ Barcelona 51, popular disco, on some weekends with live music.

The Tourist Office keeps a list of addresses of the numerous **diving organizations** in the area. Trips on **glass-bottomed boats** can be booked directly on the harbor.

Preserved marine animals (fish, starfish, corals) are sold in the souvenir shop **Mar de Coral**, C/ Santa Anna 68.

LLORET DE MAR

Serveis de Turisme, Pl. de la Vila 1, tel. 972 364735, tel 972 367750.

Roger de Flor, Turó de l'Estelat s/n, tel. 972 364800, fax 972 371637, an oasis of peace high above the town, lovely garden with pool. **Santa Marta**, Pl. de Santa Cristina, tel. 972 364904, fax 972 369280, comfortable hotel outside town, on a quiet beach.

Marsol, Passeig Jacint Verdaguer 7, tel. 972 365754, fax 972 371205, advantages of this somewhat anonymous hotel include its location directly on the beach promenade and the pool on the roof.

Miramar, Passeig Jacint Verdaguer 6, tel. 972 364762, fax 972 364586, simple and anonymous, but central and partly with sea views.

Can Bolet, C/ de Sant Mateu 6, tel. 972 371237, good Catalan seafood cuisine in the midst of this fast food jungle. **Cala Banys**, C/ Cala Banys, nice and quiet terrace café on a small rocky bay. **Jimmy's**, C/ Sant Roma 24, for snacking on tapas.

Casino de Lloret, C/ dels Esports 1, tel. 972 366512. As well as the usual casino business, in summer there are also music shows and cabarets. Those overcome with dance mania will simply fall from one disco into the next on **Av. Just Marlés**.

El Relicario, C/ Na Marina 1, flamenco / salsa shows.

Centro Cultural Verdaguer, Passeig Jacint Verdaguer, open villa with old furniture and mosaic floors, in which there are occasional art exhibitions. Open Tue-Sun 10 am-1 pm and 4-7 pm.

BOAT TRIPS can be booked at the kiosks on the beach.

Water World, May to mid-Sept: 10 am-7 pm daily, Carretera Vidreres-Girona, 1.2 km. The aquatic park with giant slides will guarantee childish happiness. Free transfer from the bus station.

PALAMÓS

Patronat de Turisme, Passeig del Mar 8, tel. 972 600550.

Trías, Passeig del Mar s/n. tel. 972 601800, fax 972 601819, a classic in the hotelscape of Palamos, situated on the beach promenade, well-equipped for handicapped people.

La Fosca, Passeig de Fosca 24, pleasant guest house on eponymous beach.

La Gamba, Pl. Sant Pere 1, tel. 972 314633, elegant seafood restaurant offering imaginative creations. **Maria de Cadaqués**, C/ Tauler i Servià, tel. 972 314009, for over 60 years this has been, and still is, a very popular place for regional specialties.

The most popular **music bars** are situated around the Plaça Sant Pere.

Diving station Nautilus Sub, Carretera Club Náutico s/n, tel. 972 316249.

PALS

Patronat de Turisme, C/ Aniceta Figueres 6, tel. 972 667857, fax 972 667818.

Mas de Torrent, Torrent (5 kilometers outside Pals), tel: 972 303292, fax 972 303293, an 18th-century estate which was very tastefully reconstructed into a luxury hotel. With pool, tennis courts and golf course.

Sa Punta, Platja de Pals (sandy bay, 5 kilometers northeast of Pals), tel. 972 667376, one of the best seafood restaurants on the Costa Brava, with 20 luxurious guest rooms, closed mid-Jan to mid-Feb and every Monday.

Cypsela, C/ Rodors 7, tel. 972 66 76 96, very well-equipped, lots of greenery, even a hairdressers salon and riding stables, closed Oct to mid-May.

PERATALLADA

Oficina de Turisme, C/ la Roca 2, tel. 972 634034.

Castell de Peratallada, Pl. del Castell, Peratallada, tel. 972 634021, fax 972 634011, exclusive ambience in a castle.

La Riera, Pl. Les Voltes 3, tel. 972 634142, fax 972 635040, guest house with medieval flair.

La Roca, C/ dela Roca s/n, friendly garden-restaurant, local cuisine.

Poblat Ibèric, near Ullastret, June-Sept: Tue-Sun 10:30 am-1 pm and 4-8 pm, Oct-May: Tue-Sun 10 am-12 pm and 4-6 pm. **Casa-Museu Castell Gala Dalí**, in Púbol on the road to Girona, July-Sept: 10:30 am-7:30 pm daily, March-June and Oct: Tue-Sun 10:30 am-5:30 pm.

PLATJA D'ARO

Patronat de Turisme, Mossén Jacint Verdaguer 11, tel. 972 817179, fax: 972 825657.

Columbus, Passeig de Mar 100, tel. 972 817166, fax 972 817503, comfortabe hotel on the beach promenade, with many extras. **Sant Jordi**, Carretera de Palamós, tel. 972 652311, fax 972 652576, out of the way of the bustle, two bathing bays stretch out below the elegant gardens.

Planamar, Passeig Maritim 85, tel. 972 817177, fax 972 825662, simple but well-maintained hotel with a pool on the roof.

🅢 **Marina,** Ciutat de Palol 3, tel. 972 817182. Quiet guest house near the beach.

🆇 **Big Rock,** Barri de Fanals 5, tel. 972 818012, this restaurant cooked itself up a Michelin star with its unusual and imaginative creations.

🎵 **Palladium**, Carretera Circumval.lació s/n. Disco, not only for the young.

🏛 **Aquadiver**, aquatic park with an abundance of attractions, Carretera Circumval.lació s/n, Open June-Sept: 10 am til sundown daily, bus transfer from bus station.

PORT DE LA SELVA

🅸 **Oficina de Turisme**, C/ Mar 1, tel. 972 387025.

🅱🅱 **Porto Christo,** C/ Major 54, tel. 972 387062, fax 972 387529, well-maintained middle-class hotel with diving school.

🅢 **Tina,** C/ Major 15, tel. 972 387149, friendly guest house, also a few apartments.

🆇 **Ca L' Herminda,** L'Illa 3, tel. 972 387075, solid Catalan cuisine.

🏛 **Sant Pere de Rodes**, Serra de Roda, about 10 kilometers from town. June-Sept: 10 am-7 pm daily, Oct-May: 10 am-1 pm and 3-5 pm daily.

ROSES

🅸 **Oficina de Turisme**, Av. de Rhode 101, tel. 972 257331, fax 972 151150.

🅱🅱🅱 **Almadraba Park**, Pl. d'Almadraba, 4 km southeast of town center. Tel. 972 256550, fax 972 256750, stylish, all mod cons, on beautiful bay.

🅱🅱 **Mediterráneo**, c/ Quevedo s/n, tel. 972 256300, fax 972 254910, comfortable, on the promenade.

🅢 **Rom,** C/ Trinidad 35, tel. 972 256181, friendly guest house in the old town.

🆇 **Hacienda El Bulli**, Cala Montjoi, tel. 972 1504 57. One of the best restaurants in the country, famous for its fantastic culinary creations. **Flor de Lis**, C/ Cosconilles 47, tel. 972 254316. This German-Swiss team shines with its exquisite cuisine.

🏛 **Bahía de Roses**, on the road to Cadaqués, aquatic park with slides, white-water canals etc. This park is designed for excitement, and not just for the kiddies! Open June to Sept. Departure times of free transfer buses from Roses can be obtained in the tourist office.

SANT FELIU DE GUIXOLES

🅸 **Patronat de Turisme**, Pl. Monestir 54, tel. 972 820051, fax 972 820119.

🅱🅱🅱 **Hostal La Gavina**, Pl. Rosaleda s/n, S'Agaro (2 km north of Sant Feliu), tel. 972 321100, fax 972 321573, luxury hotel with distinguished guest list.

🅱🅱 **Plaça**, Pl. del Mercat, tel. 972 325155, fax 972 821321, new hotel in central location. **Hostal del Sol**, Carretera de Palamós 194, tel. 972 320193, fax 972 820677, Art Nouveau villa in enchanting garden, with pool.

🆇 **Can Toni**, C/ Garrofers 54, tel. 972 321026, exquisite cuisine in understated surroundings, closed Tuesdays and from Oct to May. **Cau del Pescador**, C/ Sant Domènec 11, tel. 972 324052. Delicious seafood.

🚶 The HIKE up to **Ermita de Sant Elm** is well worth the effort, if for nothing else then for the glorious view over the cork oak forests and the town of Sant Feliu.

TAMARIÚ

🅸 **Oficina de Turisme**, C/ Riera s/n, tel. 972 620193.

🅱🅱-🅱🅱🅱 **Hesperia Hostalillo,** C/ Bellavista s/n, tel. 972 620228, fax 972 620184, pleasant hotel with fantastic views over the bay.

🅱🅱 **Tamariú**, Passeig del Mar 3, tel. 972 620031, informal hotel on beach promenade.

TOSSA DE MAR

🅸 **Oficina Municipal de Turisme**, Av. del Pelegri 25, tel. 972 340108, fax 972 340712.

🅱🅱🅱 **Rey Mar,** Platja Mar Menuda. tel. 972 340312, fax 972 341504, comfortable hotel in beautiful location directly on the beach.

🅱🅱 **Diana**, Pl. de Espanya 6, tel. 972 341886, fax 972 341103, an Art Nouveau treasure on the promenade, although slightly overpriced considering the modest standard.

🅢 **Palmera,** C/ la Guàrdia 29. tel. 972 340249, fax 972 340089, guest house close to beach, with small pool.

🆇 **Es Moli**, C/ Tarull 3, tel. 972 341414, lovely garden-restaurant with superb cuisine and high prices. **Bahía**, Passeig del Mar 19, tel. 972 340322, popular seafood restaurant on the beach promenade.

🎵 **Vila Vella**, by the old town walls below the fort, lovely terrace bar with views of Tossa. **Catxa-Club**, Carretera Sant Feliu (1.2 kilometers outside town, to the north), open-air disco with pool.

🏛 **Museu Municipal**, Pl. Roig i Soler 1, in summertime from Tue-Sun 10 am-6:30 pm, in winter Tue-Sun 10 am-1 pm and 3-6 pm.

🚤 Excursions on **glass-bottomed boats** are available from a whole range of organizers at the beach.

🤿 **Centro de Submarinismo**, Mar Menuda. tel. 972 341000. Diving lessons and equipment rental.

Costa Brava

BARCELONA –
THE CAPITAL OF
CATALONIA

BARRI GÒTIC
EIXAMPLE

Barcelona

**BARCELONA
History**

Catalonia's capital city of **Barcelona** veritably overflows with dynamic energy. Commercially it ranks as number one in Spain, but this metropolis of 1.5 million inhabitants has always pointed the way for the rest of the country, whether in the areas of culture, architecture, or art and design. Events important in Barcelona's development were the World Exhibitions of 1888 and 1929, as well as the Olympics in 1992 which resulted in the harbor and sea being, so to speak, "claimed back" for the city; old warehouses and run-down industrial complexes were razed and in their place beautiful boulevards lined with cafés, restaurants and museums were created. However, the city administration is by no means resting on its laurels. Many new projects including the restoration of several old town quarters, road development, extension of the airport and further links to the high-speed rail system AVE are already in full swing.

Barcelona's history began on the hill of Mont Tabor, where the cathedral stands today. This is where, in the 1st century

Left: The cathedral of Barcelona – Gaudís "unfinished masterpiece".

B.C., the Romans founded the settlement of *Julia Augusta Paterna Faventia Barcino.* In the 4th century the region was Christianized and by the 5th century the town had become a fairly important political and religious center under Visigoth rule. At the beginning of the 8th century it was captured by the Moors, but was already liberated by Luis I, the Pious, by 801. In 898 Guifré el Pelós united the Catalan nations of the county of Barcelona, which won independence from Carolingian rule in the 10th century. The marriage in 1137 of Ramón Berenguer IV, the Count of Barcelona, to the heiress of the kingdom of Aragón, resulted in Barcelona becoming the capital of the new kingdom of Aragón-Catalonia and ensured rapid promotion of the town to one of the leading trade and marine metropolises in the Mediterranean. Following the unification of Castile and Aragón in 1479 through the marriage of Ferdinand II of Aragón and Isabella I of Castile, Barcelona lost its commercial and political position to Seville. In the Spanish War of Succession (1701–1714) the Catalans sided with the Habsburgs, who were defeated by the Bourbons. From then on, Barcelona was held back both politically and commercially, and didn't begin to profit from trade with the Americas and Spanish colonies until the monopoly was lifted in 1778. In the middle of the 18th century Barcelona flourished as a prosperous industrial center, due to the building of the first Spanish railway line, from here to Mataró. Throughout the Spanish Civil War (1936–1939) Barcelona remained a Republican stronghold. Following the victory of Franco, Catalonia was forced to give up its autonomy, the presidents of the *Generalitat* (Catalan government) were all executed and all things Catalan were suppressed until the dictator's death in 1975. In 1979 Catalonia's autonomy was reinstated and in 1980 Jordi Pujol, who is still in government to this very day, was elected president of the *Generalitat*. 1992 was undoubtedly Barcelona's big year, with its hosting of the 25th Olympic Games. It basked in the spotlight and received world attention once more in 1997, when Cristina de Borbón married Basque handball star, Inaki Urdangarín, in the city's cathedral.

**BARRI GÒTIC – The Old Town

The true heart of old Barcelona beats in its Gothic quarter **Barri Gòtic (Spanish: *Barrio Gótico*) and innumerable buildings provide evidence for the medieval glory and wealth of this royal trading center. During the day its narrow streets are mostly visited by rushing tourists and its true character does not shine until after the sun has gone down, when the entire quarter sparkles in gently-floodlit illumination. This is when the locals themselves come out and enjoy the atmosphere of their old town, in its numerous street cafés and bars.

The magnetic center of attraction in the Barri Gòtic is the magnificent **Cathedral ❶ (*Seu*), which succeeded its Romanesque predecessor church in 1298. On its huge forecourt, the Plaça de la Seu, locals meet up every weekend (Saturdays at 6:30 pm, Sundays at 12 pm) to dance the *Sardana* – a round dance

which has always been representative of the confidence and pride of the Catalans. The western façade of the Cathedral, which faces the Plaça, wasn't fully completed until the 19th century, whereas the most important parts of the building were already finished in 1498. One typical characteristic of Catalan Gothic architecture is the complete absence of an outer buttress. The supporting columns are located inside, and the spaces in between them are taken up by opulently-furnished chapels. The harmonious Gothic vault of this three-aisled church is carried by mighty beam-pillars. As is usual in Spanish cathedrals, the choir area blocks the view from the middle aisle onto the apse. The filigree woodcarvings of the choir stalls date back to the 14th/15th centuries and the coat of arms of the Order of the Golden Fleece are emblazoned across the seat rests. A broad staircase leads down into the crypt, in which the graceful marble sarcophagus of the patron saint of Barcelona, St. Eulàia, rests. The reliefs on this magnificent sarcophagus as well as the scenes tastefully carved into the marble wall of the choir, depict the terrible martyrdom of the saint. Beneath the altars the Gothic panel by Bernat Martorell (around 1450), dedicated to the theme of Christ's Transfiguration, stands out. Through the southern portal – a relic from the Romanesque predecessor church, the way leads in to the "green oasis" of the cloisters. Here, visitor's cameras instinctively point at the unexpected geese happily waddling about, whose original job was more than likely the protection of the cathedral treasury from the more butter-fingered visitors, by means of their vehement cackling.

The Carrer Bisbe Irurita leads past the **Palau Episcopal ❷ (bishop's palace) and through the Roman city gates with their round towers, and heads straight for the **Plaça de Sant Jaume**. With the Palau de la Generalitat de Catalunya, the seat of

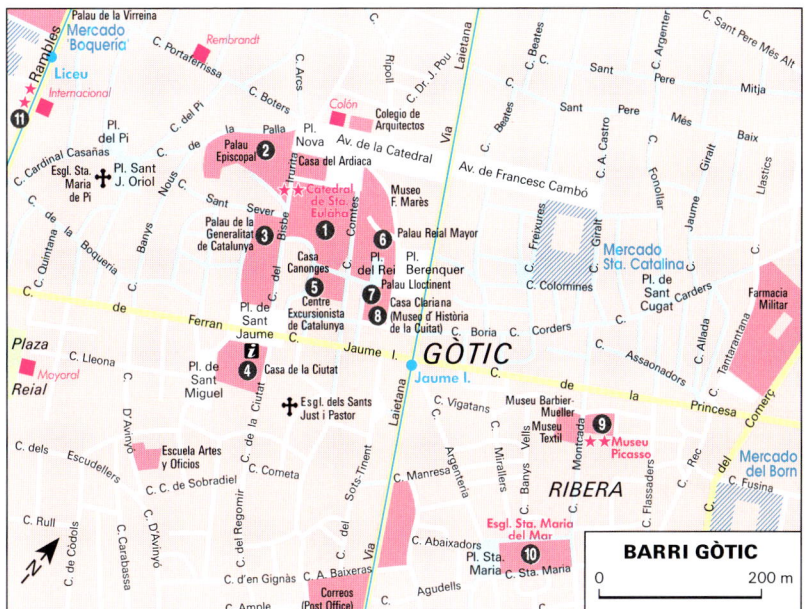

Barcelona

the autonomous government of Catalonia, and the Casa de la Ciutat, the town hall, the square which dates back to the Roman forum is to this very day the political center of the city.

The origins of the **Palau de la Generalitat** ❸, with its Gothic inner courtyard and chapel of Sant Jordi, date back to the 15th century, but the main façade of the building in Renaissance-style did not originate until the 17th century. The neo-Gothic crossing over the Carrer Bisbe Irutita connects the Generalitat building to the former **canons' residences**, which today serve as the residence of the president of Catalonia.

Behind the classical façade of the **Casa de la Cuitat** ❹ (town hall) you'll find the famous **Saló de Cent meeting rooms** – the meeting room of the Council of Hundred, which was opened in 1373. In the Middle Ages, the Jewish quarter (**Call**) of Barcelona used to be situated west of the seat of the *Generalitat*. Little remains to remind us of it today. The pretext for completely destroying this quarter in the

14th century is that the Jews had supposedly been responsible for bringing the plague into the city.

The narrow Carrer Paradis leads from the Plaça de Sant Jaume to the headquarters of the Catalan hiking club **Centre Excursionista de Catalunya** ❺, which in its interior houses the remains of an Augustine temple dating from around 100 A.D.

Past the apse of the Cathedral the Baixada de Sta. Clara leads on to the architecturally-cohesive **Plaça del Rei** (king's square), which buskers have selected as their favorite spot due its superb acoustics. The Plaça is dominated by the **Palau Reial Major** ❻ (king's palace) and its striking watch tower, in which the Counts of Barcelona and later the Kings of Aragón once resided. The former throne room, the **Saló de Tinell**, with its daring vaulted construction, is where Colombus was received by the Catholic monarchs following his voyage of discovery, in 1493. The palace chapel, **Sta. Àgata**, dating from the 14th century, contains the altar painting *Retrat del Condestable* (1464/65), a masterpiece by Catalan artist Jaume Huguet. Also on the Plaça del Rei you'll find the **Palau del Lloctinet** ❼, the 16th-century palace of the viceroy, containing the archive of the crown of Aragón. In the museum of history next to the palace, the **Museu d'Historia de la Ciutat** ❽, the old Roman town was unearthed during excavation work, the remains of which may be viewed in the museum's basement.

You can reach the quarter of **Ribera** via the Via Laietana. In the Middle Ages Ribera used to be the domain of merchants, craftsmen and seafarers. On the splendid boulevard **Carrer de Montcada**, the aristocracy and wealthy Patricians once resided, but today the time-honored palaces mainly accommodate museums and art galleries. In the Palau Aguilar and Palau del Baró de Castellet (15th century) the **✶✶Museu Picasso** ❾ now resides, in which the artist's various periods are superbly depicted. The exhibition displays gifts to Picasso and the *Collection of Jaume Sabartés,* who was both his friend and secretary. Paintings which particularly stand out are *The Harlequin* (1917) and *Portrait of the Señora Canal* from his "pink", as well as the 58 artworks from the *Meninas* series.

At the end of Carrer de Montcada you come to the **Sta. María del Mar** ❿, which is a perfect example of pure Catalan Gothic architecture. The 14th-century church is very impressive due to its clear lines, the quality of light in its interior and the apparent transparency of its architectural components, emphasized by the surprisingly stylized octagonal columns.

Around the ✶✶Ramblas

Along the ✶✶**Ramblas** ⓫, Barcelona's lively pedestrian zone stretching from the

Right: Nocturnal activity in the cafés along the Ramblas.

Plaça del Catalunya all the way to the harbor, there is always something going on – day and night. Mime artists, musicians and dancers all do their best to attract a crowd. There is a constant hubbub, which in itself is entertainment enough. The colorful goings-on are best viewed in comfort from one of the many street cafés. Today's Ramblas is situated on a former river which ran dry in the 15th century. And this is where the name *Ramblas* originated – as it derives from the Latin Arenno (river bed) and was developed into Rambla by the Arabs. The use of the plural is the result of this boulevard being divided up into five sections, which each radiates its own individual charm.

The spaciously-designed **Plaça de Catalunya** ⓬, one of the most important traffic intersections in the entire city, forms the starting point for a stroll along the Ramblas. At first this tree-lined boulevard falls under the name **Rambla de Canaletes**, but beyond a cast iron fountain (from which, it is said, those who drink will return once more to Barcelona) it's called **Font de Canaletes**. In the 19th century, during the modernist era, it was considered very chic to keep birds as pets and since then birds have been on sale on the **Rambla dels Ocells**. Beneath the former baroque Jesuit church, the **Església de Betlem**, the **Rambla de Flors** commences with its innumerable flower stalls. The most magnificent palace along the Ramblas was once home to the viceroy of Peru. Today, the former **Palau de la Virreina** ⓭ houses the Department for Cultural Affairs, which occasionally displays short-term exhibitions on a whole variety of themes.

Whatever you do, try not to miss a visit to the ✶**Boquería Market** ⓮ – nowhere else in Barcelona will you come across such an incredibly wide and seductive range of delicious fruit and vegetables!

A slight detour in an easterly direction will lead you to the **Plaça del Pi** (pine plaza), which is reputed to be one of the

most beautiful plazas in the entire city. A touch of Bohemian flair permeates the atmosphere, particularly when artists offer their work for sale here on Saturdays. The bars around the Gothic church **Sta. María del Pi** , from the 14th century, appear very inviting for indulging in a touch of idleness. Another major sight along the Ramblas is the famous opera house **Gran Teatro del Liceu** , which was re-opened in 1999 following extensive restoration of severe damage caused by fire.

A little further on, on the left-hand side, you'll see the **★Plaça Reial** (royal plaza), an enclosed arcade-lined classical plaza. Innumerable cafés and restaurants beckon the visitor to take a break, and on Sundays the plaza becomes a meeting place for stamp and coin collectors. Opposite, in the Nou de la Rambla, the once-privileged quarter of the wealthy was to be found. This is where Eusebi Güell had a modernistic city palace, the **Palau Güell** , designed by none other than Antoni Gaudí, who also designed the in-

terior. It interior, which has remained the original, is open for viewing,

The infamous **Barri Xino**, the entertainment and red-light district close to the harbor area, was polished up in recent years and several dubious establishments were forced to close down. It is apparent that this quarter is in the process of being made a little more respectable.

Barcelona's Old / New Harbor

Columbus, the legendary seafarer and discoverer, thrones upon a 60 meter-high column at the end of the 1.5-kilometer Ramblas, surrounded by a barrage of busy traffic. In the interior of this **Monument a Colom** , an elevator rises to a viewing platform from which you can enjoy a good view of the harbor and city.

The medieval boatyards **★Reials Drassanes** remind us of Catalonia and Aragóns great seafaring history. Today the Gothic halls of these time-honored boatyards house the shipping musuem, the **Museu Marítimo**. The modern industrial harbor of Barcelona today lies to the southwest, beneath Montjuic.

The old harbor was completely redesigned for the 1992 Olympics – the result of which was very well received. The **Moll de la Fusta** ㉑ (wooden mole) was converted into a palm-lined promenade of exclusive restaurants and cafés. A wooden bridge leads to the pier, **Moll d'Espanya,** with the hyper-modern shopping and entertainment center of **Maremàgnum** and a spaciously designed **aquarium**. The **Moll de la Barceloneta** also underwent beauty treatment: in the once-largest warehouse which today bears the name **Palau del Mar** the **Museum d'Historia de Catalunya** was installed, in which the history of Catalonia is, didactically speaking, very clearly illustrated. The quarter of **La Barceloneta**, which stretches out on a peninsula, is a popular spot, particularly because of its superb seafood restaurants. The **Platja de Barceloneta**, the city dwellers' local beach, is packed to bursting at the weekends. Walking along the beach in a northerly direction you'll come to the **Vila Olímpica**, a modern residential complex with numerous sports facilities built in 1992, and to the **Olympic Port Nova Icária** and a popular boulevard of bars and discotheques.

From the Passeig de Colom, running parallel with the Moll de la Fusta, the trip continues to the **Església de la Mercè** ㉒. This late baroque 18th-century basilica is the residence of the Virgen de la Mercè, or patron saint of the city, in whose honor a lavish celebration is held annually on 24th September. Further east you'll find the **Llotja** ㉓, the old 14th-century stock exchange featuring a neo-classical façade. The **Parc de la Ciutadella** ㉔ borders on the quarter of Barceloneta. It is located on the grounds of Philipp V's citadel. Situated within the gardens are the Catalan Parliament, several museums and the city **zoo** ㉕.

Montjuic and the Olympics

The 213-meter-high hill of **Montjuic** ㉖ is one of the most popular recreation areas here and offers a whole range of cultural and recreational activities. But this was not always the case: for a long time the hill served only as a military base. Today the presence of the **Castell** ㉗ bears evidence to this history. It was built in the 17th century and originated as a fortress which Philipp IV built in 1640 to keep the unpredictable Catalans in check. Today the fort houses the **Museu Militar**, but the main attraction here is the glorious view over the city and the sea.

The northern entrance to Montjuic is the **Plaça d'Espanya** ㉘ with its two

large brick towers reminiscent of the tower of St. Marco in Venice, which formed the gateway to the 1929 World Exhibition.

On the Avinguda de la Reina María Cristina, the exhibition establishments are literally lined up, but the crowning glory of this majestic street is the monumental national palace with its ★**Museu Nacional d'Art de Catalunya** ㉙. The Romanesque Catalonian frescoes make for a particularly unique collection and a highlight for art aficionados. The **Font Magica** ㉚, which thanks to special lighting effects transforms into a magical fountain in the evenings and a somewhat kitschy feast for the eyes, gushes forth in front of the national palace.

The somewhat hidden **Pavelló Mies van der Rohe** (a faithful copy of the original) lies further uphill. Created by German architect Mies van der Rohe as Germany's contribution for the World Exhibition of 1929, its pavilion and interior are considered perfect examples of Bauhaus design.

All of Spain and its greatest sights are represented in the **Poble Espanyol**, in miniature. At night the open-air museum with its bars and discos becomes a social spot for Barcelona's youth.

Another attraction on Montjuic is the ★**Fundació Joan Miró** ㉛ (Miró Foundation), designed by Josep Lluís Sert, which presents the Catalan artist's work in a most impressive way. Above the museum on the **Anella Olímpica** (Olympic circle), built especially for the 1992 Olympic Games, there are several sports complexes. The **Estadi Olímpic** (Olympic stadium) dates back to 1929. The steel-grilled construction of the Olympic hall, **Sant Jordi**, was designed by Japanese architect Arata Isozaki and still serves as a multi-purpose building. The white, futuristically-inclined **radio tower** is a piece by the famous Valencian star architect Santiago Calatrava.

The visit to Montjuic ends stylishly with a cable car ride, **Transbordador Aéri** ㉜ (Tue-Sun 12-8 pm). From the Miramar platform it glides down over the harbor as far as the beach of Barceloneta.

EIXAMPLE – Quarter of Modernism

Modernism – the artistic emblem of Barcelona borne of Art Nouveau, developed with the *Renaixença* – revival of the Catalan culture. The extension of the city during the second half of the 19th century was orchestrated by Ildefons Cerdà, who offered Antoni Gaudì and Lluís Domènech i Montaner the opportunity to realize their creativity, which is why most modernistic buildings are located in Eixample.

The privileged of the city preferred to set up home along the majestic boulevard of **Passeig de Gràcia**, which to this day has remained the finest and most exclusive shopping and entertainment street in all of Barcelona. The most beautiful palais are in **Quadrat d'Or**, or "golden square", between Carrer d'Aribau and Passeig de Sant Joan. The most famous group of houses on Passeig de Gràcia is the **Mançana de la Discòrdia**, the "block of discord". This derisive description comes from the contrasting building designs. The **Casa Lleó Morera** by Lluís Domènech i Montaner shows the then brand-new inventions such as the tele-

Right: On the roof of the Casa Milà.

phone, gramophone, camera and lightbulb as decorative external elements. Right next door is the **Casa Amatller** built by Josep Puig i Cadafalch for a chocolate factory owner. The stepped, Flemish-style gable roof is decorated with colored tiles; the most contrasting style elements are harmoniously united here. The most original Patrician house, the **Casa Batlló**, is the work of Gaudí. Its roof of scalloped ceramic tiles is supposed to resemble the dragons from the legend of St. George. It is not without reason that the modernist artists repeatedly cited Sant Jordí, as St. George is the patron saint of Catalonia. The façade reveals Gaudí's playful nature regarding both form and material and this building is a creation of his lively imagination.

The **Casa Milà** which is one block further and stands on the opposite side of the street, is a large apartment building. It too carries the signature of the extremely individual genius. It didn't take long for this massive building to be christened with a new name in colorful common parlance: it is known as *La Pedrera* or "heap of rubble". As far as the quality of living is concerned, Gaudí certainly was ahead of his time. The house has a built-in air conditioning system, an underground car park and apartments which can be individually redesigned thanks to adjustable walls. A Gaudí museum has just been set up on the top floor and the original roofscape is open for viewing once again.

Carrer Majorca, which is a little out of the way, is the location of Gaudís masterpiece and Barcelona's most famous landmark: the **★★Temple (Expiatorti) de la Sagrada Familia** ([Atonement]Temple of the Holy Family). Between 1910 and 1926 – the year of his death, Gaudí dedicated all of his creativity and energy to this building, which since its very beginning has been supported solely by donations. Its completion date remains unforeseeable. This house of god is particularly impressive because of its outer façade

and individual statistical elements: Gaudí's parabol arch and the complexity of the religious symbolism complement each other in quite a unique way.

Discoveries in the Outskirts

★Parc Güell is a 20-hectare oasis situated on Barcelona's outskirts, far removed from the hectic bustle of the city. Eusebi Güell commissioned Gaudí with the establishment of a garden city in 1910, but potential buyers exhibited little purchasing interest and when the First World War broke out Güell abandoned the ambitious project. The town hall, with its 84 worryingly crooked-looking columns, was meant to be the center of the complex and is one of the few parts of it which were actually completed. In the only completed house, in which Gaudí himself once resided, there is a museum with personal memorabilia and furniture which belonged to the famous architect.

North of **Tibidabo** and next to the **Sagrado Corazón** church, you'll come to an inviting amusement park. A historical old tram, the **Tramvia Blau**, is an option which can ease your upward journey. A walk through the beautiful forest, with many stunning views of the city always from a different perspective, is an alternative to a stroll in the aforementioned park. The architect Norman Foster implemented new architectural styles with his design of the radio and observation tower on Barcelona's second hill – the **Torre de Collserola**.

Another gem left over from Gothic Barcelona can be found on the edge of town. The **★Monestir Santa Maria de Pedralbes** was founded by Queen Elisenda de Montcada in 1326. Thanks to the speed of the building of the church, cloisters with three galleries and monastery buildings all represent a perfectly uniform homogeneity. The final resting place of its founder can be found in the presbyterium beside the main altar and in one of the wings 80 paintings from the Thyssen-Bornemisza collection are on display.

BARCELONA

Turisme de Barcelona, C/ Tarragona 149-157, tel. 934 231800, fax 934 232649. **Oficines d'Informació Turística**, Aeropuerto de El Prat, tel. 933 255829, fax 934 784736, Mon-Sat 8 am-8 pm, Sun and holidays 8 am-3 pm; Casa de la Ciutat, Pl. de St. Jaume I, Mon-Fri 9 am-9 pm, Sat 9 am-2 pm; Estació Sants, Pl. dels Països Catalans, Mon-Sat 8 am-8 pm, tel. 934 914431; Gran Vía de les Corts Catalanes 658, tel. 933 017443. Issuing office for the **Barcelona card** (valid for 1-3 days) which grants discounts for museums, sights and some public transportation, is at: Metro junction, Pl. de Catalunya 17, underground, tel. 933 043135.

AIRPORT: 14 km outside the city in **Prat de Llobregat**. Flight information, tel. 933 013993. Rail connection from Barcelona-Sants station every 30 mins between 6 am and 10 pm. Buses run from Pl. de Catalunya every 15 mins, Sundays and holidays every 30 mins. *METRO* (subway): The ticket is valid for the entire subway network but not for the Generalitat rail line. Cards valid for 10 trips are cheaper. *TRAMVÍA BLAU* (blue tram): from Av. Tibidabo, Balmes to Pl. Dr. Andreu, runs half-hourly. *CABLE CAR*: **Funicular Tibidabo**, from Pl. Dr. Andreu, 7:30 am-9:20 pm daily. **Funicular Montjuic**, from Av. Paral.lel to Av. Miramar, in summer from Mon-Sat 11 am-10 pm, Sun 12-2:45 pm and 4:30-9 pm. **Funicular de Vallvidrera**, from Av. Vallvidrera to Pl. P. Ventura. **Transbordador Aeri del Port**, from the harbor Torre Sant Sebastiá via Torre Jaume I to Jardins de Miramar, Montjuic, 11 am-6:45 pm daily, from June to Sept 11 am-10 pm daily. **Teleferico de Montjuic**, from Av. Miramar on Montjuic to Castell de Montjuic. *GOLONDRINAS* (boats): departure from the Columbus monument, March-Oct 10 am-8:30 pm daily; trip to the mole takes only 15 mins. *RAIL STATIONS:* **Estación Central**, quarter of Sants, Pl. Països Catalans. **Estación de Francia**, Passeig Nacional. **Estación Cercanías** (local trains), Passeig Nacional. Information tel. 934 900202. *BUS STATIONS:* **Julia** (to Germany, France, England, Switzerland, Scandinavia, Italy and Portugal), Pl. Universitat 12, tel. 933 183895. **Iberbus** (to France, Belgium, Holland, Italy), Av. Paral.lel 116, tel. 933 296406. **Alsina i Graell** (to Andorra), Rda. Universitat 4, tel. 933 026545. **Les Courriers Catalans** (to Paris), C/ Pau Clarís 117, tel. 933 025875. *PORTS:* **Estación Baleares**, Moll de les Drassanes. **Estación Internacional**, Moll de Barcelona. *RENTAL CARS:* **Avis**, C/ Casanova 209, tel. 932 099533. **Hertz**, C/ Tusset 1, tel. 932 373737. **Atesa**, C/ Balmes 141, tel. 932 378140. **Europcar (Interrent),** C/ Viladomat 214, tel. 934 398403. **Rental Auto**, Av. Sarrià 32, tel. 932

309071. *MOTORBIKES:* **Vanguard**, C/ Londres 31, tel. 934 393880.

Le Meridien Barcelona, Ramblas 111, tel. 933 186200, fax 933017776, stylish, for more sophisticated needs. **Rivoli Ramblas**, La Rambla 128, tel. 933 026643, fax 933 175053, friendly art-déco-style hotel. **Colón**, Av. Catedral 7, tel. 933 011404, classic hotel, cathedral views. **Hesperia**, C/ Los Vergos 20, tel. 932 045551, quiet location. **Espanya**, C/ Sant Pau 9-11, tel 933 181758, fax 933 171134, dining room and foyer designed by modernist architect Puig i Cadafalch. **San Augustí**, Pl. de San Augustí 3, tel. 933 181658, comfortable hotel in quiet location. **Mayoral**, Pl. Real 2, tel. 933 179534. **Montserrat**, Passeig de Gràcia 115, tel. 932 172700. **Paseo de Gracia**, Passeig de Gràcia 102, tel. 932 155824. **Montecarlo**, Ramblas dels Estudis 124, tel. 934 120404, fax 933 187323, central location. **Gaudí**, C/ Nou de la Rambla 12, tel. 933 179032, conservative. **Astoria**, C/ Paris 203, tel. 932 098311, fax 932 023008, good breakfast buffet. **Hostal Windsor**, Rambla de Catalunya 84, tel. 932 151198, bright, friendly atmosphere. **Jardi**, Pl. Sant Josep Oriol 1/Pl. del Pi, tel. 933 015958, fax 933 183664, simple, but excellent location on Pl. del Pi. **La Equitativa**, Passeig de Gràcia 44, tel. 932 159300, well-kept, simple rooms.

CATALAN: **Can Massana**, Pl. del Camp 6. **Agut**, C/ Gignás 16. **Agut d'Avignon**, C/ Trinitat 3. **El Petit Dorado**, C/ Dolors Moncerdá 51. **Florian**, C/ Beltrand i Serra 20. **Gargantúa i Pantagruel**, C/ Aragó 214. **Gran Colmado**, C/ Consell de Cent 318. **Barceloneta**, C/ Escars 22.

SEAFOOD: **Casa Chus**, Av. Diagonal 339. **Senyor Parellada**, C/ Argentería 37. **Can Majó**, C/ Almirante Aixada 23. **Çan Culleretes**, C/ Quintana 5.

SPANISH: **Azulete**, Via Augusta 281. **La Balsa**, C/ Infanta Isabel 4. **Cas Isidro**, C/ Flors 12. **La Troballa**, C/ Riera San Miguel 69. **Botafumeiro**, C/ Gran de Gràcia 81, Galician, high quality. **Elche**, C/ Vila i Vilá 71, Valencian.

BASQUE: **Triton**, C/ Alfambra 16. **Amaya**, La Rambla 20. **Gorria**, C/ Diputacio 421.

VEGETARIAN: **Illa de Gracia**, Domenec 15. **Macrobiotico Zen**, Muntaner 12. **Govinda**, Pl. Villa de Madrid 4-5.

DISCOS: **Distrito Distinto**, Av. Meridiana, 104. **Studio 54**, Av. Paral.lel 54. **Up and Down**, C/ Numancia 179.

MUSIC BARS: **Els Quatre Gats**, C/ Montsió 5 (Jazz). **Sisisi** (Jazz), Av. Diagonal 442. **Este Bar**, C/ Consell de Cent 257. **Frank Dube**, C/ Buscarons 24. **Humedad Relativa**, Pl. Mañe i Flaquer 9. **King Bar**, Av. Diagonal 618. **Mas i Mas**, C/ María Cubí 199 (St. Gervasi).

BARCELONA

Metropol, Passage Domingo 3. **Mirablau**, Pl. del Funicular, Mirasol, Pl. del Sol 3. **Nick Havanna**, C/ Roselló 208 (Eixample). **Particular**, Av. Tibidabo 61 (Sarriá-St. Gervasi). **Universal**, C/ María Cubí 182-184 (St. Gervasi). **Velvet**, C/ Balmes, 161 (Eixample). **Zig-Zag**, C/ Platón, 13 (Sarriá, St. Gervasi).

FLAMENCO: **Bandolero**, C/ Muntaner 244. **El Patio Andaluz**, C/ Anibal 242. **El Cordobés**, Rambla Caputxins 35. **Blanca Paloma**, C/ Napols, 222.

MUSEUMS ON MONTJUIC: **Fundació de Joan Miró**, Tue-Sat 11 am-7 pm, Thur until 9:30 pm, Sun and holidays 10 am-2:30 pm. **Museu d'Art de Catalunya**, Tue-Sat 10 am-7 pm, Sun and holidays 10 am-2:30 pm. **Museu de la Ceramica** and **Museu de Artes Decorativas**, Av. Diagonal 686, Palacio de Pedralbes, Tue-Sun 10 am-2 pm. **Museu Arqueológico**, Tue-Sat 9:30 am-1:30 pm and 3:30-7 pm; Sun and holidays 10 am-2 pm. **Museu Ethnológico**, Wed and Fri-Sun 10 am-2 pm, Tue and Thur 10 am-7 pm. **Museu Militar**, Castell de Montjuic, Tue-Sun 9:30 am-1:30 pm and 3:30-7:30 pm.

MORE MUSEUMS: **Museu Picasso,** C/ Montcada 3-5 pm, Tue-Sat 10 am-8 pm, Sun 10 am-3 pm. **Museu Barbier-Mueller** (pre-Columbian art), C/ Montcada 14, Tue-Sat 10 am-8 pm, Sun and holidays 10 am-3 pm. **Museu-Monestir de Pedralbes** and part of Thyssen-Bornemisza collection, Baixada del Monestir, Tue-Sun 10 am-3 pm (metro: Palau Reial). **Museu Textil i de L'Indumentaria** (traditional costumes), C/ Montcada, Tue-Sun 10 am-5 pm, Sun and holidays 10 am-2 pm. **Museu d'Art Modern**, Parc de la Ciutadella, Mon-Sat 9 am-9 pm. **Museu de la Ciéncia**, C/ Teodor Roviralta 55, Tue-Sun 10 am-8 pm. **Casa Museu Gaudí**, C/ Olot (in Parque Güell), Sun-Fri 10 am-2 pm and 4-7 pm. **Museu del Teatre**, Nou de la Rambla 3 (in Gaudí's Palau Güell), closed for renovation. **Museu de la Historia de la Ciutat**, Tue-Sat 10 am-2 pm and 4-8 pm, Sun 10 am-2 pm, Aug-Sept 10 am-8 pm daily. **Museu Maritim**, Pl. Portal de la Pau 1, Wed-Fri 9:30 am-2 pm and 4-7 pm; Tue and Sat 9:30 am-1 pm and 4-7 pm; Sun and holidays 10 am-2 pm. **Museu de la Música**, Av. Diagonal 373, Tue and Thur-Sun 10 am-2 pm, Wed 5-8 pm, in modernist building by Puig i Cadafalch. **Museu d'Art Contemporaní**, Pl. dels Àngels, Tue-Sat 11 am-2 pm and 4-8 pm, Sun 10 am-3 pm. **Museu Clara**, C/ Calatrava 27-29, Tue-Sun 9 am-2 pm. **Museu Frederic Marés**, C/ Comtes de Barcelona, Tue-Sat 10 am-5 pm, Sun 10 am-2 pm. **Museu del Perfum**, Paseig de Gràcia 39, Mon-Fri 10:30 am-1:30 pm and 4:30-8 pm, Sat 10:30 am-1:30 pm Uhr. **Museu de Zoología** (in 1888 Expo building, by Domènech i Montaner), Paseig del Tillers, Tue-Sun 10 am-2 pm. **Museu Futbol Club Barcelona**, Arístides Maillol, Estadio C.

F. Barcelona, Mon-Fri 10 am-1 pm and 3-6 pm, Sat/ Sun 10 am-2 pm. **Museu Diocesá**, Pl. de la Seu 7, Tue-Sat 10 am-1:30 pm and 5-8 pm, Sun 11 am-2 pm.

SIGHTS: **Pavelló Mies van der Rohe** in exhibition park by Montjuic, 10 am-6 pm daily. **L'Aquàrium**, Maremagnum, 9 am-9 pm daily, July/Aug. 9 am-11 pm daily. **Casa de los Canónigos**, C/ del Bisbe. **Centro Excursionista de Catalunya**, C/ Paradís 10. **El Gran Teatre del Liceu**, Rambla de Caputxins, 61. **Fundació Tàpies**, C/ Aragó 255, Tue-Sun 11 am-8 pm. **La Font Mágica** (fountain), Pl. Carles Buigas, shows Thur and Sat/Sun 9 pm to midnight, in winter Sat/Sun 8-11 pm. **Llotja** (Lonja), Passeig de Isabel II. **Palau (Palacio) de la Música Catalana**, C/ Amadeu Vives 1, modernist building by Domènech i Montaner. **Palau Reial Mayor** with Saló de Tinell, Tue-Sat 10 am-2 pm and 4-8 pm, Sun and holidays 10 am-2 pm. **Parc Güell**, C/ Olot, 10 am-6 pm daily. **Poble Espanyol**, Av. Marques de Comillas, Parc de Montjuic, 9 am-8 pm daily, in winter until 6 pm (restaurants are open longer). **Temple de la Sagrada Familia**, Pl. de la Sagrada Familia, 9 am-7 pm daily. **Zoo**, Parc de la Ciutadella, 9:30 am-7:30 pm daily. **Columbus Monument**, Tue-Sat 10 am-2 pm and 3:30-6:30 pm, Sun 10 am-7 pm.

CHURCHES: **Cathedral** and **museum,** Tue-Sat 10 am-2 pm and 3-8 pm, Sun 11 am-2 pm. **Sta. María del Pi(no)**, 8:30 am-1 pm and 4:30-9 pm daily. **Sant Pau del Camp**, Mon-Fri 10 am-1 pm and 4-6 pm, Sat/Sun 10 am-1 pm. **La Mercè**, 9 am-2 pm and 5-7 pm daily.

Post office (Correu Central): Pl. Antoni López, Mon-Fri 8 am-10 pm, Sat 9 am-8 pm, Sun 9 am-11 pm.

23.4.: *Sant Jordi* (St. George), patron saint of Catalonia. **11.5.**: *Fiesta Sant Ponç*, herb and natural foods market in C/ del Hospital. **24.6.**: *San Juan*, the 23rd to 24th is celebrated all night long in the streets. **11.9.**: *Diada*, Catalan National Day. **24.9.**: *Virgen de la Merced*, patron saint of Barcelona. Around the **15.8.**: Fiesta in the Gràcia quarter of town.

Bullfights, not very popular in Catalonia, every Sunday from April to October in Barcelona: Pl. de Toros Monumental, Gran Vía Corts Catalans, 747.

Fashion: Elegant fashions and jewelry on Passeig de Gràcia between Pl. de Catalunya and Av. Diagonal, other fashions in C/ Aragón and C/ Valencia. Rambla de Catalunya, Av. Diagonal between Passeig de Gràcia and Pl. Francesco Macia and northern side streets, upper C/ Muntaner. **Antiques**: Centro de Anticuarios, Passeig de Gràcia 55. **Handicrafts**: Artespaña, Rambla de Catalunya 75. **Second-hand bookshops**: Mercado del Libro, Mercant de Sant Antoni, Sun 10 am-2 pm. **Markets**: La Boquería, Rambla de San José. Mercado de Sant Antoni, C/ Urgell. Mercat des Sants, C/ Sant Medir, C/ Cáceres.

Barcelona

57

THE COSTA DORADA

COSTA DEL GARRAF
NORTHERN COSTA DORADA
TARRAGONA
SOUTHERN COSTA DORADA

Costa Dorada

COSTA DORADA

The coastline from Calafell to the Ebro delta and belonging to Tarragona province is known as the **Costa Dorada**. Touristically speaking it is a very important region and is famous for its large sandy beaches, which are said to shimmer like gold (Catalan: *Dorada*) in the sunlight.

Until a few years ago the coastline south of Barcelona, which still belongs to Barcelona province, was considered part of the Costa Dorada. In the meantime though, it has received its own name and discovered its own identity – as the **Costa del Garraf**. An eponymous barren mountain ridge forms the boundary of this flat coast, protects it from cool winds and, last but not least, gave it its name.

Beside the tourist ghettos there are also pretty areas and stunning hinterlands to be explored on these southern Catalan coasts, as is the case on the Costa Brava farther north, and it's well worth a journey of discovery.

Tarragona, the capital town of the province, was one of the most important cities

Previous pages: The baroque parish church of San Bartomeo dominates the main beach of Sitges. Left: The election of the Wine Queen is a highlight of the Festa de la Verena.

on the Iberian peninsula in Roman times. Nowadays it proudly promotes itself with remnants from its rich history. But this modern industrial and commercial town is everything but an open-air museum. On the contrary, it is a bustling, lively town, exuding Mediterranean flair.

Between almond and hazelnut plantations, mighty, medieval monasteries in wild and empty expanses of landscape beyond the coast, such as Poblet and Santes Creus, remind us of Catalonia's great Cistercian age.

COSTA DEL GARRAF

Castelldefels ❶, with its beach 5 kilometers in length, has long been a popular recreation destination for the inhabitants of Barcelona and one of the great capital's dormitory towns.

Behind the town the coastal road winds uphill and affords majestic views of the Costa del Garraf, the pearl of which is undoubtedly ***Sitges ❷**, a holiday resort which can actually still be described as a "seaside resort" in the old-fashioned sense. The turn-of-the-century architectural fabric, including many Art Nouveau villas along the beach promenade, **Passeig Maritim**, lends the town its distinctive character. But Sitges is by no means an antiquated, dusty old town.

Quite the contrary: despite its "Belle-Époque" backdrop it presents itself as a surprisingly lively and outward-looking place. Today the young, unconventional clientele feels at home in this town, where once only well-heeled Catalan summer visitors were to be found. Last but not least, the European "gay scene" has found its niche here.

The town developed modestly from the Roman harbor of *Subur* in the Middle Ages and towards the end of the 19th century it became quite famous thanks to a group of outdoor painters, the *Sitges-Luminists.* Santiago Rusiñol (1861-1931), a representative of Catalan Art Nouveau otherwise known as *modernism,* purchased two fishing houses in the old town and transformed them into an artistic center. Just like Dalí's house in Cadaqués on the Costa Brava, Rusiñols *Cau Ferrat* became a beloved meeting-place for artists during his lifetime and, after his death, a museum. The **Museu Cau Ferrat** exhibits artworks by mainly Catalan artists, as well as Rusiñol's own rather unusual collection of wrought-iron exhibits, but also includes Picasso's *Bullfight* (1901) and two of El Greco's pieces, whose rediscovery in the 20th century was considerably influenced by Rusiñol himself.

Together with the **Museu Maricel** next door, which houses a small but exquisite collection of medieval art and a collection of nautical instruments, Cau Ferrat is one of the gems of this whitewashed old town sitting on the rocky outcropping of **La Punta** and is bounded by the main beach and the Platja Sant Sebastià, and dominated by the town's baroque church.

But above all it is the original tapas bars, fine restaurants, chic boutiques and the legendary, lively nightlife which attracts a colorful mix of holidaymakers.

Further attractions throughout the year include a transvestite carnival in February, the *Festival of Fantastic Films and Horror Films,* a theater, jazz and tango

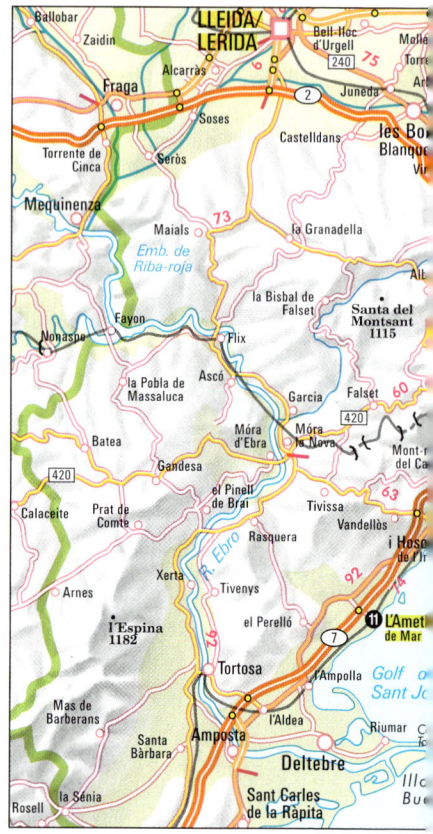

festival as well as the wine festival *Festa de la Verena* in September.

But what would a seaside resort be without its beaches? 2.5 kilometers of fine sand, divided into 17 sections each with a different name, are located right on the doorstep. The **Platja de Sant Sebastià,** an extension of these beaches, is situated beyond the town to the north.

The industrial town of **Vilanova i la Geltrú**, 8 kilometers southwest of here and the result of two individual towns merging together, has an entirely different character. The 12th-century **Castell de la Geltrú**, in which the city museum is housed, is the dominating building in the **La Geltrú** part of town, to which the *Vilanova* or "new town" was annexed.

Info p. 72-73

Tourism plays only a minor role here. Many visitors appreciate its cheap rates of accommodation (in comparison with Sitges), its traditional fishing quarter and good value seafood restaurants on the **Passeig Maritim**. Those not satisfied with the modest beaches can drive on to Sitges.

The Penedès

Wine enthusiasts tend to go into raptures when they hear the word **Penedès**. Viniculture has been popular in this region since the time of the Romans. Toward the end of the 18th century the success story of the Penedès began and today it is the most famous of the registered wine growing areas *(Denominació d'Origen)* in Catalonia.

Vilafranca del Penedès ❸, the main town of Old Penedès, lies amidst lush vineyards. The Plaça Jaume I with its **Santa Maria** parish church, an example of Catalan Gothic, is evidence of the medieval significance of this place. The royal palace opposite, **Palau Reial**, built in the 13th century and once home to several royal couples, demonstrates architectural severity. Today, amongst other exhibitions, it is the home of the **Museu del Vi(no)**. Before tasting any wines it is worthwhile finding out more about the history of viniculture in this region.

A destination for wine pilgrims is the winery of **Miguel Torres**. This renowned wine growing dynasty operates branches in Chile and California and produces one of the most highly-decorated Spanish wines. Before you personally sample the wines, which range from palatable whites to heavy reds, you should partake in a bus tour around the extensive vineyard.

Those not being obliged to take the wheel themselves during this trip are truly blessed, because only a few kilometers away in the town of **Sant Sadurni d'Anoia** ❹ (10,000 inhabitants) the thrilling highlight of this wine trip awaits. This is where 95 % of all sparkling Spanish wines from over 100 vineyards are produced, including *Freixenet* and *Codorníu*, best known in Europe. Almost all the wineries offer sightseeing tours and tastings. One must though, is a visit to *Can Codorníu*, where the history of Spanish sparkling wine began 120 years ago (see feature on page 82). At the end of each tour, the corks are popped and the day ends in a seventh heaven of sheer *Cava* bliss.

NORTHEASTERN COSTA DORADA

The border between the two provinces of Barcelona and Tarragona lies close to the small resort of **Cunit** and, from here on, the coast is known as the Costa Dorada.

Calafell ❺ developed from an Iberian settlement, which was founded 2500 years ago and destroyed by the Romans. Several years ago archaeologists presented the town with a new attraction when they excavated the settlement and reconstructed it. A trip through the houses, workshops and worship rooms of the ✶**Ciutadella Ibèrica** paints a clear and vivid picture of the lifestyle of the old Iberian culture.

Right: Expert wine tasting – superb wines, which can be sampled on one of your vineyard visits, are produced in Penedés.

The pretty old town is also worth visiting. It is crowned by a castle, under the protection of which is a Romanesque parish church with the still-preserved remains of Early Roman frescoes, and it is also home to a beautiful beach.

The traffic intersection of **El Vendrell** ❻, off the coast, is above all else famous for its great Catalan cellist Pau (Pablo) Casals (1876-1973). A monument to him on the main square, just a few meters from his birthplace, recalls the life of this convinced anti-fascist, who spent the years following the Civil War and up to his death in exile out of protest against Franco's regime. An exhibition in the **Casa-Museu Pau Casals**, the family's own summer house in the **Sant Salvador** part of town, recalls the life and work of the musician. Music festivals which take place here in August attract audiences from all around the globe.

The second best-known suburb of El Vendrell, **Coma-ruga**, is particularly popular with camping tourists due to its wide and almost white beach.

The road on which the modern traffic of today pushes its way toward Tarragona is the very same road on which many years ago Roman carriages rushed by at breakneck speed. The historical **Via Augusta**, an imperial military highway which stretched all the way from Gaul into southern Hispania, can still be made out thanks to visible evidence on the roadside 20 kilometers before Tarragona. The **Arc de Berà**, a legacy from the Roman period, is a highly impressive triumphal arch 10 meters in height, which was raised as a monument to Consul Lucius Licinus Sura during the time of Trajan in the second century.

Three towns which all have historic roots and retained their own individual charm despite growing tourism, are Torredembarra, Altafulla and Tamarit, which are literally lined up next to each other. International hotels will hardly be found here and the holiday apartments

and camp sites are mainly frequented by natives during the holiday season.

Torredembarra is divided in two by the N 340 highway. The real town center lies to the north and the holiday settlements with their usual, interchangeable touristic infrastructure lie alongside the sea. But also by the sea is the small fishing quarter of **Baix a Mar** and the old town, which sits on a hill. Water lovers will appreciate the beach of **Platja del Barri Marítim**, which is several kilometers long, wide and boasts fine sand.

The fishing town of **Altafulla** with its pretty **Platja d'Altafulla** and walled old town center does survive mainly from tourism, but appears to have remained peaceful and modest. The excavated Roman settlement of **Els Munts** in the municipal district illustrates the grand old age of this town.

Tamarit de Mar ❼, selected in the 12th century by the archbishop of Tarragona as his summer retreat, has always remained a favorite summer spot for many of Tarragona's inhabitants. The medieval **Castell de Tamarit** rises picturesquely upon a rock and the Romanesque chapel of **Sant Martí** above the beach is reminiscent of the days of *Reconquista.*

**TARRAGONA

Tarragona ❽ (115,000 inhabitants) is the capital of the eponymous province and the second-largest city in Catalonia, after Barcelona. In Roman times it was the other way around: *Tarraco,* capital of the province of *Hispania Tarraconensis,* far outweighed its northern counterpart both in power and influence. It was the temporary residence of Caesars Augustus and Hadrian and with its population of 30,000 was one of the most important metropolises in the Roman empire. It remained important throughout the Middle Ages as an archbishopric, even when the region's political power was transferred to Barcelona.

New town quarters and industrial areas have clustered themselves around the

foot of the old town hill. Today Tarragona is an influential harbor city and center of the petrochemical industry. Yet it can still offer its inhabitants the flair of an historical city, a higher standard of living than most resorts towns and employment.

The **old town,** the charming *Casc Antigua*, is not only the realm of day-trippers. It is inhabited and doesn't appear antiquated in the slightest. Here, it is the locals who dominate the bars and restaurants and the chic and traditional stores. The Roman ruins, which you'll come across time and again when strolling through the town, are not attractions in the sense that they can only be admired if the appropriate admission fee has been paid: they serve as peaceful areas of relaxation which form a very real part of the modern cityscape.

The city wall surrounds most of the old town. Behind the 18th-century outer wall there is an older one, made up of huge megalithic blocks and ashlars from varying periods of Roman rule and the Middle Ages. The **★Passeig Archeològic ❶**, an

archaeological walking path in park-like design, runs between the double fortification from the Portal del Roser to the Portal de Sant Antoni and so leads around part of the old town.

Most of the innumerable temples, opulent villas and baths dating from Tarraco's golden era, have been damaged or destroyed right down to their foundations. In recent years their remains coincidentally glimpsed the light of day during building projects and they were subsequently excavated. Such as at the **Plaça del Fòrum ❷** where remains of the provincial forum can be made out. From here you navigate your way through the narrow lanes of **El Call**, in which the medieval Jewish community of Tarragona had its quarter, to the Plaça del Rei with its **Castell del Rei** – the royal castle otherwise known at the praetorium. This may well be the remains of the palace of the Roman praetors, which was converted into a royal residence in the Middle Ages. Today it is the home of the **★Museu d'Historia de la Ciutat** (city museum) and in the new building next door you'll find the ★★**Museu Nacional Archeològic** ❸ (national archaeological museum). Both display findings from ancient Tarraco including mosaics, sculptures and sarcophagi.

The **Plaça de la Font** was partly built over the **Circ Romans** ❹ (Roman circus) in the 19th century, of which practically nothing remains. It's hard to imagine that 23,000 spectators enjoyed their beloved chariot races at this very spot. In its place, the lively old town square offers modern entertainment in the form of bars and restaurants.

The highest point in town, where a temple to Jupiter, a Visigoth church and a mosque once stood, is the site of the ★**Catedral Santa Tecla** ❺. Its building began in the 12th century and it was consecrated in 1331. St. Thekla, patron saint of the town, is honored annually on 23rd September with lively celebrations.

The church belongs to the most beautiful of those built in the Roman-Gothic style. Both medieval styles intermingle visibly on the main portal. While the Roman side portals duck modestly, the elegant, French-style Gothic apostles decorate the architraves and are, together with the Madonna in the middle, a gentle contrast to the drastic vision of hell in the tympanum. A beautiful rosette bathes the light of the interior in a mystical aura and dominates the façade of unfinished towers.

The interior is entered through the interesting cloisters, which were built at the end of the 12th century in the place of an orange yard belonging to the previous mosque. Today, it presents itself once again as a masterpiece of Arabian garden landscaping, because the square between the columned walkways of this Mediterranean garden has been beautifully transformed by orange trees, climbing roses and acanthus blossoms. Both round and pointed arches harmonize perfectly and, like the monks in medieval times, you can

stroll along the walkways of capitals which depict medieval fantasies, immortalized forever in stone.

The side capitals function as viewing rooms for the superbly-designed ★**Museu Diocesà,** which features Roman and Moorish exhibits, and of course also Christian art.

The church interior itself forms part of the museum and contains the most priceless piece of all, the **main altar** (15th century) which is made of alabaster. The predella depicts scenes from the life of St. Thekla.

The **amphitheater** ❻ rises outside the old town walls. 12,000 spectators used to watch animal and gladiator fights in this arena, in front of the glittering Mediterranean.

If you're exhausted from all the sightseeing you could take a rest on the local beach of **Platja del Miracle**. The popularity of this beach has remained unaffected by the fact that the poor quality of water in this part of town leaves a lot to be desired.

The **Rambla Nova** ❼ forms the centerpoint of the new town, which was not established until the 19th century at the foot of the old town hill. Cafés and shops line the boulevard which leads straight to the **Balcó del Mediterrani,** a viewing platform offering panoramic views of the harbor area.

On the road to Lleida, 6 kilometers outside town, an ★**aquaduct** crosses the 1st-century *Puent de Diable* ("devil's bridge" according to locals) and a broad valley. It serves as an impressive example of the ingenious design of the Roman water system. Two rows of water arcades, one built over the other, carry water along its journey at a height of 27 meters.

Reus is first and foremost a trade center for agricultural produce, and also a shopping town. Most visitors to the Costa Dorada only ever see the airport of this town, over which all the charter flights are carried out. But this lively town is also

Costa Dorada

known as the birthplace of two famous Catalan artists: the painter Marià Fortuny (1838-74) and the Art Nouveau architect, Antoni Gaudí.

SOUTHERN COSTA DORADA

The true touristic centers of the Costa Dorada, Salou and Cambrils, are situated south of the refinery complexes of Tarragona. The monument to the conqueror Jaume I rises proudly on **Salou's** ❾ elegant palm-fringed promenade, the **Passeig de les Palmeres,** which runs along the entire east beach and was designed in the style of the *Promenade des Anglais* in Cannes. The Phocaeans built the harbor from which the conqueror and king is said to have set sail for the Balearic island of Majorca. Salou has the appearance of an elegant seaside resort with many Art Nouveau villas from its

Above: The cathedral of Tarragona – a successful combination of Romanesque and Gothic style elements.

early days lining the **Calle Jaume I** which runs alongside the promenade. This is where the fine Catalan art of strolling can be practised and friends can be made whilst rollerblading. The numerous hotels and restaurants stretching for kilometers up to Cap Salou and Cambrils in the south, have adapted to the tastes of the average holidaymaker. The main beach, **Platja de Llevant**, is situated behind the promenade which is partly shaded by pine trees and hopelessly overcroweded in summertime. Similarly overcrowded but just as well-maintained and fine-grained are its smaller neighboring beaches and also the long **Platja Llarga** in the east, which is sectioned off by several pretty bays. Almost every sport is available here and the popularity of Salou is undoubtedly due to its fine beaches.

A new attraction lent this town's crumbling popularity new impetus a few years ago: **Port Aventura**. In this amusement park you can go on a trip around the world, from the Mediterranean to the Wild West via China. This project cost over 250 million dollars and was opened in 1995. Its aim was to provide Euro-Disney with some worthwhile competition. The stable climate here was surely an advantage and the superlative amusement rides and shows meant that success was imminent.

Like Salou, the neighboring town of **Cambrils** ⑩ was discovered as a potential tourist town in the late 1960's. Both of these towns have long since grown together. But while Salou has irrevocably sacraficed itself in the name of tourism, Cambrils has remained more modest. Its main attraction is its fishing harbor, but even a yacht club has been added to keep the tourists happy.

The main beach, **Platja Regueral i Prat d'en Forès**, is lined by a promenade. All the other beaches reaching all the way to Salou are relatively small in comparison and are, in parts, bordered by the main road.

Parc de Samà, 3 kilometers outside the town center, possesses some beautiful walking paths amidst its fine tropical and Mediterranean vegetation. It was designed for the Samà i de Torrents family in the 19th century by the famous landscape architect Josep Fontseré, as a reminder of their stay on Cuba and the Philippines.

Those visitors wishing to avoid the hubbub should drive further southwards to **L'Ametlla de Mar** ⑪. The vast, finely-grained beaches of northern Costa Dorada simply don't exist here, but instead, sand and pebble bays lined with pine trees and evergreen shrubs have free spaces for beach towels, even in summer. At the same time the unique atmosphere of this small fishing community can be explored. *La Cala* (bay) is what the locals call it, an indication of its natural harbor which once protection to seafarers. In the late afternoons it is a relaxing pleasure to watch the fishing boats coming in and observe the auctioning of the catch in the nearby hall.

The Cistercian Triangle

Almond and hazelnut plantations and a few olive groves characterize the landscape between Tarragona and **Lleida**, which appears to be void of human life. This is where the Cistercian monks of the Middle Ages chose to retreat to in order to establish their mighty monasteries, such as those in Poblet and Santes Creus.

The reformation order of Cistercians was mainly influenced by St. Bernard of Clairvaux (1090-1153), who preached for a "reinstatement of monastic roots, the ideals of St. Benedict" and who fought furiously against the decadence taking place in many of the monasteries during the Middle Ages. **★★Santes Creus** ⑫ dates back to 1150 and was one of the first in a whole series of Cistercian monasteries which were founded in Catalonia. The site chosen was a remote valley which would provide adequate peace and quiet for worship, penance and contemplation.

The simple Romanesque portal of the **monastery church** dominates the Plaça Major with its baroque abbey, which today serves as the community's town hall. A ring of battlements provides evidence that this church also had to attend to duties of defense.

Its interior, the fabrication of which commenced at the end of the 12th century, radiates peace and grandeur. There is no superfluous curlicue, as the Cistercians were averse to every kind of pomposity, even in their architecture, and only the splendid Gothic graves serve as a reminder that during the 13th and 14th centuries Santes Creus was the burial site of two generations of Kings of Catalonia-Aragón.

One highlight of the monastery complex is the **"new" cloisters**. Dating from the second half of the 13th century, the majestic work on the pointed arches depicts the *flamboyant* style in all its perfec-

Costa Dorada

tion. However, the figure capitals are completely in the Romanesque style. Bernard of Clairvaux, the ultimate puritan, would surely not have approved of the fantastical creations by British designer Reinard des Fonoll: between saints and biblical figures he allowed bagpipe-playing fools, a monkey riding on a dromedary and mythical creatures to all make an appearance.

On the eastern side of the cloisters you'll find the entrance to the hall of capitals, in which influential abbots found their final resting places. A set of steps leads up to the dormitories, the roof of which is supported by eleven mighty pointed arches.

The Napoleonic Wars left Santes Creus badly damaged. It was plundered following secularization in 1835 and since its restoration has become a museum featur-

Above and right: Sta. Maria de Poblet, established in the 12th century as a symbol of victory over Islam, and its monastery church designed in typical Cistercian simplicity

ing a multimedia show dedicated to the history of the Cistercian order.

Quite unlike Santes Creus, the monastery of Santa Maria de Poblet to the northwest is once again inhabited by about 30 monks, who uphold Catalan Cistercian traditions. The way to Poblet leads over the small medieval town of ***Montblanc** ⓭. Behind its almost perfectly-preserved town walls and amid the confusion of angled lanes the mighty church of **Santa Maria La Major** (14th century) rises up. Given its baroque portal, this church provides quite a surprise, because its interior is pure Catalan Gothic.

**Santa Maria de Poblet ⓮ was founded in 1151 as a show of triumph over the Moorish enemy. The originally simple Cistercian building was rebuilt several times over the centuries. Generous donations made for the creation of a grand complex worthy of serving as the burial site to several generations of Kings of Catalonia-Aragón. For some time Poblet was actually one of the richest and mightiest monasteries in all of Europe.

Costa Dorada

The monastery complex is made up of three unwalled areas. The outer area was reserved for laymen who supported the monastery's policy of self-sufficiency with their crafts and agricultural skills. The Late Gothic chapel is a veritable treasure. It was dedicated to St. George, better known as the famous dragon slayer or San Jordi, patron saint of Catalonia, toward the middle of the 15th century by Alfonso The Magnanimous.

The 15th-century **Porta Dorada** leads into the second area which centres around a spacious square, the Plaça Major. Even the greatest kings made their way past the Romanesque **Capilla de Santa Catalina** on foot. The simple 14th-century **Porta Reial** leads into the innermost part of the monastery, which is protected by imposing walls.

Even to this day, the Romanesque cloister is in practical use by the monks and, like the monastery's library, is not open to the public. But the spirit of the Middle Ages can also be felt in the **"new" cloisters**, which is yet another fine exam-

ple of the transitional style of Romanesque to Gothic. A haven of peace and meditation was successfully established around the hexagonal fountain house. Weave patterns, floral motifs and arabesques decorate the capitals of the columned walkways.

The three-aisled **monastery church**, the building of which began in 1170 and was not completed until the 14th century, leads into a choir aisle with a chapel circle. The choir area is filled by an alabaster retable by Renaissance artist Damià Forment, which blends harmoniously into the Romanesque structure. But the elements here which dominate most everything else are the sarcophagi of Alfonso The Chaste, Pere The Conqueror, Martin The Humanist and Pere the Ceremious and their spouses, which depict Catalonia's great age. The invaluable graves were victimized by plundering which took place in the 19th century, but were restored to their former state in 1940 thanks to the care and intuition of sculptor Frederic Marès.

ALTAFULLA

ℹ Oficina de Turisme, Pl. dels Vents s/ n, tel. 977 650752, fax 977 650008.

🏛 Vila Romana dels Munts, Mon-Sat 10 am-1:30 pm and 4-7:30 pm, in winter Mon-Sat 3-5:30 pm.

CALAFELL

ℹ Oficina de Turisme, C/ Sant Pere 29-31, tel. 977 699141, fax 977 692981.

🛏 ⊙⊙⊙ Miramar, Rambla Costa Dorada s/n, tel. 977 690700, comfortable hotel situated close to the beach.

⊙⊙ Canada, C/ Mossèn Jaume Soler 44, tel. 977 691500, fax 977 691255, simple hotel with pool.

⊙ Salome, C/ Monturiol 19, tel. 977 690100, fax 977 692382, basic hotel with garden, situated close to the beach.

❌ L'Ancora, Av. Sant Joan de Déu, tel. 977 694777, international and Catalan cuisine, on the beach promenade.

🍸 Discotheques and bars are mainly to be found in the area around the streets of **C/ Vilamar** and **C/ Monturiol**.

🏛 Ciutadella Ibèrica, Carretera 246 to Barcelona, near the disco Louie Vega, open mid-June to mid-Sept from 10 am-2 pm and 5 pm until sunset, daily; during the rest of the year from 10 am-2 pm and 4 pm until sunset, daily.

CAMBRILS

ℹ Oficina de Turisme, Pl. Creu de Missió s/n. tel. 977 361159, fax 977 794572.

🛏 ⊙⊙-⊙⊙⊙ Centurion Playa, C/ Diputacion 70, tel. 977 361450, fax 977 361500. Older but newly-renovated house in excellent location direction on the beach between Cambrils and Salou. **Monica**, C/ Galverán Marquet 1-3, tel. 977 360116 or 977 791000, fax 977 793678, pleasant hotel with shady gardens and pool, only 50 meters from the beach.

⊙⊙ Rovira, Av. Diputació, tel. 977 360900, fax 977 360904, with sea views. **Port Eugeni**, on the harbor, tel. 977 365261, fax 977 360057, with pool.

⊙-⊙⊙ Tropicana, Av. Diputació, tel. 977 360112, fax 977 360112, simply-furnished hotel with pretty gardens, separated from the beach only by the road.

❌ Can Gatell, Passeig Miramar 27, tel. 977 360057. Well-known seafood restaurant, higher prices. **La Roca d'en Manel**, Passeig Miramar, good fish and good prices.

🏛 Parque Sama, 3 kilometers outside town on the road to Montbrío, open from 9 am until one hour before sundown, daily.

EL VENDRELL

ℹ Oficina de Turisme, C/ Dr. Robert 33, tel 977 660292, fax 977 665924.

🏛 Casa-Museu Pau Casals, in the harbor quarter of Sant Salvador, April-Sept: Tue-Sun 11 am-2 pm and 5-8 pm, Oct-May: Tue-Sun 11 am-2 pm.

L'AMETTLA DE MAR

ℹ Oficina de Turisme, Sant Joan 55, tel. 977 456477, fax 977 456838.

🛏 ⊙ Bon Repos, Pl. Catalunya 49, tel. 977 456025, simple but attractive hotel with pool and garden.

MONTBLANC

ℹ Oficina de Turisme, Pl. Major 1, tel. 977 860009.

🛏 ⊙ Ducal, C/ Diputació 11, tel. 977 860025, simple and inexpensive.

SALOU

ℹ Oficina de Turisme, Xalet Torremar, Passeig Jaume I 4, tel. 977 38350102, fax 977 380747, and C/ Montblanc 1, tel. 977 380136.

🛏 ⊙⊙-⊙⊙⊙ Cap Salou, Cala de la Font 1, tel. 977 371985, fax 977 370301, middle-class hotel on the outskirts, very close to a small bay. **⊙⊙ Donaire Park**, Pl. de Rec s/n, tel. 977 371066, fax 977 371150, both families and young people will feel at home in this lively beach hotel. **Negresco Princess**, C/ Replanells s/n, tel. 977 370392, fax 977 370393, beautiful location on a cliff plateau on the outskirts of town, 400 meters to the sandy bay. **Cala Font**, Cala de la Font, tel. 977 370 454, fax 977 371804, good location on a quiet bay.

🎢 Port Aventura, superlative recreation park, Av. Pere Molas, 2 kilometers along the A7, exit 35, 26th March-1st Nov: 10 am-8 pm daily; 20th June-13th Sept: 10 am-midnight daily, bus connections from Salou and other towns.

SANT SADURNI D'ANOIA

ℹ Oficina de Turisme, Pl. de la Vila, tel. 938 8911212.

🍷 CAVA WINERIES: Can Codorníu, C/ Caseriu s/n, tel. 938 911162, Mon-Fri 10 am-6 pm. **Freixenet**, C/ Joan Sala 2, tel. 938 911162, Mon-Fri 9 am-1 pm and 3-7 pm, pre-booking preferred.

SITGES

Patronat Municipal de Turisme, C/ Sínia Morera s/n, tel. 938 944251, fax 938 94 43 05.

San Sebastian Playa, Port Alegre 3, tel. 938 948676, fax 938 940430, Belle Époque hotel with lots of flair and all the usual modern conveniences, situated directly on the beach promenade of Platja Sant Sebastià.

Celimar, Passeig de la Ribera 20. tel. 938 110170, fax 938 110403, Art Nouveau hotel with modern interior on the beach promenade.

Subur, C/ Espanya 1. tel. 938 940066, fax 938 946986, modern hotel close to the beach which attracts a young and active clientele. **Romàntic**, Sant Isidre 33, tel. 938 948375, fax 938 948167, a bit antiquated, but lovingly furnished and very romantic.

Rivamar, Passeig de la Ribera, 46, tel. 938 943408, solid guesthouse on the beach promenade.

Mare Nostrum, Passeig de la Ribera 60, tel. 938 943393, regional specialties, lots of seafood dishes. **Amore**, Passeig de la Ribera 18, tel. 938 944104, cheap, for fans of paella and fideuà. **Izarra**, C/ Mayor 22, tel. 938 947370, beautiful tapas bar with Basque specialties, in the pedestrian zone.

There are several **discotheques** in the area around C/ Bonaire and C/ Sant Pau. Many **gay bars** around C/ Bonaventura. *CASINO:* **Gran Casino Barcelona**, near Sant Pere de Ribes on the road to Vilafranca del Penedès.

Museu Cau Ferrat and **Museu Maricel**, C/ Fonollar s/n, Tue-Fri 9:30 am-2 pm and 4-6 pm (in winter only 4-6 pm), Sat 4-8 pm, Sun 9:30 am-2 pm. **Museu Romàntic**, C/ Sant Gaudenci, Tue-Sat 9:30 am-2 pm and 4-6 pm, Sun 9:30 am-2 pm.

POBLET

Monestir, Les Masies de Poblet, tel. 977 870058. Simple rooms, nice views of the monastery.

Monestir Santa Maria de Poblet, 10 am-12:30 pm and 3-6 pm, in winter until 5:30 pm.

SANTES CREUS

Monestir de Santes Creus, 10 am-1 pm and 3:30-7 pm, in winter until 6 pm. Exciting multimedia show, several languages.

TARRAGONA

Patronat de Turisme, C/ Fortuny 4, tel. 977 233415 and C/ Major 39, tel. 977 241935.

Imperial Tarraco, Rambla Vella 2, tel. 977 233040, fax 977 216566. The beautiful sea views and 4-star comfort make up for the somewhat boring architecture.

Hotel Urbis, C/ Reding 20, tel. 977 240116, fax 977 243654, friendly little middle-class hotel in the new town, centrally located, free parking.

España, Rambla Nova 49, tel. 977 232712, simple and inexpensive.

Les Coques, Baixada del Patriarca 2, tel. 977 228300, Catalan cuisine in sophisticated surroundings, in the old town. **Sol Ric**, Via Augusta 227, tel. 977 233032, traditional Tarragonese cuisine and superb regional red wines. **Can Llesques**, C/ Natzaret 6 (Pl. del Rei). tel. 977 222906, Catalan snacks, young people love this place. **Bar Coimbra**, C/ Gobernador Gonzalez 6, rustic bar with solid tapas at low prices. The aperitifs should be taken next door, where good wines are served directly from the barrel.

Poetas, Sant Llorenç s/n. Beautiful music bar. Many **bars** for a younger clientele are situated in the Pau del Protectorat, west of the Rambla Nova and north of the station.

Cathedral and **Museu Diocesano**, June-Oct: 10 am-7 pm daily; Oct-May: 10 am-1 pm and 4-7 pm daily. **Passeig Arqueològic**, June-Sept: 9 am-8 pm, Oct-May: 10 am-1:30 pm and 3:30-6 pm daily, entrance on the Pl. del Pallol. **Museu Nacional Arqueològic**, Pl. del Rei, Tue-Sat 10 am-1 pm and 4:30-8 pm (in winter 6-7 pm), Sun 10 am-2 pm. **Museu d'Art Modern**, C/ Santa Anna, Mon-Fri 10 am-8 pm, Sat 10 am-3 pm and 6-8 pm, Sun 11 am-2 pm.

TORREDEMBARRA

Patronat de Turisme, Pl. dels Vents s/n, tel. 977 650752, fax 977 650008.

Paradis, C/ Camí del moro 65, tel. 977 641598. Less heavenly than its name, but nevertheless a pleasantly informal guesthouse.

VILAFRANCA DEL PENEDÈS

Oficina de Turisme, C/ Cort 14, tel. 938 920358, fax 938 921166.

Pere III el Gran, Pl. del Penedès 1, tel. 938 903100, solid middle-class hotel.

Museu del Vi (Weinmuseum), Pl. Jaume I, Tue-Sat 10 am-2 pm and 4:30-7:30 pm, Sun 10 am-2 pm.

VINEYARD TOURS: **Miguel Torres**, C/ Comercio 22, tel. 938 177400, fax 938 177444, booking recommended.

Costa Dorada

Genius and Performer

In 1964, in *Diary of a Genius,* the artist wrote: "Every morning when I awake I feel exquisite bliss: the bliss of being Salvador Dalí, and fascinated, I ask myself what wonderful things this Salvador Dalí will achieve today."

The surrealist master, one of the greatest painters of the 20th century, was certainly not lacking in self-confidence. This egocentric Catalan had a significant role to play in the development of modernism, but it was also his own sparkling personality which created strong impressions, the influence of which cannot be detached from his artistic achievements.

Salvador Dalí i Domènec, born as a notary's son in 1904, already attracted attention as a youngster through his artistic and literary talents. At the beginning of the 1920's during his education at the San Fernando art college in Madrid, from which he was expelled before graduating due to his eccentric behaviour, his friendships with Luis Buñuel and Frederico Garcia Lorca began to blossom. These relationships would have a lasting influence on Dalís development, as would those of Pablo Picasso and other surrealist artists including Paul Eluard and Max Ernst with whom he would become acquainted several years later in Paris.

Dalí received literary attention through his diverse publications which featured in several surrealistic newspapers. Together with Luis Buñuel he wrote the screenplays for the films *Un chien andalou* (1928) and *L'Age d'or* (1929).

A visit from René Magritte, Paul Eluard and his wife Gala to Dalí's home in Cadaqués in the summer of 1929

Previous pages: After a day's work this Penedès winegrower likes to sample the high quality of his own wines. Right: In front of the Dalí Museum in Figueres.

would change his life irrevocably from one day to the next. He felt irresistably attracted to the beautiful Russian, Helena Diakonoff, also known as Gala. The love affair with a married woman which followed led to a breakdown in relations with his puritanical father. Gala was to become this unstable artist's muse, model, the center of his life and his calming influence. In 1930 the couple moved into a fishing cottage in Port Lligat by Cadaqués, which over the years they converted into a truly surrealistic palace.

Dalís paintings, which were influenced in part by Freud's psychoanalyses, achieved their first acclaimed attention in the beginning of the thirties, especially pieces such as *Butterfly Landscape, The Ghost of Sex Appeal* or *Soft Watch at the Moment of First Explosion,* which belong to his many famous achievements.

Dalí did not assume a strong position nor hold any particular views regarding the problem of growing faschism in Europe, which at that time divided the intellectual arena. He described himself as an unpolitical person, but did artistically incorporated the subject in works such as *The Enigma of Hitler* and *Soft Construction with Boiled Beans.* He defended these works from the critics by describing them as attempts to understand the mysticism of Hitler from a surrealistic point of view, but his ignorance regarding the impending political situation ended up costing him his popularity with a lot of his creative counterparts.

Soon though, an exhibition in new York brought Dalí sweeping international success, which he understood very well how to convert into hard currency. But his excellent business sense introduced a lot of jealousy. André Breton once satirized Dalí by transforming the letters of his name into the anagram "Avida Dollars" and in 1939 the cord connected to the surrealist family was finally cut.

During the Spanish Civil War from 1936 to 1939, Dalí and Gala lived in exile

in Paris before resettling in America in 1940. In 1948 their homesickness led them back to Catalonia, to the Costa Brava, where Dalí remained until his death.

With time Dalís paintings depicted an ever-growing element of mysticism and spirituality. Many of his works are variations on biblical themes: *The Madonna of Port Lligat, The Temptation of St. Anthony* or *The Christ of St. John on the Cross.*

The older Dalí became, the better he understood the art of performance. One publicity gag followed another and although art critics reacted with scepticism, the public was thrilled and gave ovations. Dalí knew how to market his talents in an extremely lucrative way. With the building of the Teatre-Museu, which was opened in 1974 in his home town of Figueres, he dedicated a monument to himself.

The death of Gala in 1982 completely devastated him. The winning team was split and the maestro's inspiration ap-peared to dwindle. King Juan Carlos I showed his respect for the artist by awarding him with the title of Marquès de Púbol. In 1983 the fledgling aristocrat completed his final painting, *The Swallow's Tail,* and began his retreat from the public stage. The palace in Púbol, which he had once presented to Gala, became his home until 1984 when he was seriously injured due to a large fire. The artist sought refuge in Torre Galatea, which was linked to his theater-museum in Figueres. Dalí died there on 23rd January 1989 and, according to his wishes, was laid to rest in the museum's crypt, surrounded by his paintings and ritual objects.

The Spanish state inherited his substantial fortune and works of art, which deeply hurt the proud Catalans. The Fundació Gala-Salvador Dalí foundation still takes care of his estate and for a few years now the "surrealistic triangle" consisting of the museum in Figueres, the house in Port Lligat and the palace in Púbol, has been open for public viewing.

Any Excuse for a Celebration

Just like everywhere in Catholic Spain, highlights on the religious calendar are celebrated with enthusiasm. Every village celebrates the feast day of its own patron saint, and then there are also the national *festas* which are, according to the occasion, celebrated with a lot of Catalan tradition.

"The *Sardana* represents the essential rhythm of Catalonia – the heart dances and the head calculates". This is how the Art Nouveau artist Santiago Rusiñol described this Catalan national dance. Accompanied by the *Cobla* – a band of woodwind and brass, a double bass and a drum from which peculiar, snaring sounds emanate, people join hands, form a circle and move leisurely to complicated steps and to the rhythm of the music. The contrast to the impetuous, emo-

Above: Anyone can join in to the Sardana. People meet on Sundays in front of the Cathedral of Barcelona for this Catalan folk dance.

tionally-charged flamenco dance couldn't be more striking.

During the days of complete suppression of the Catalan culture under Franco's dictatorship, the Sardana was declared illegal by the dictator as it was a symbol of Catalan unity.

On Sundays around noon, people congregate around the Cathedral square in Barcelona to dance the sober, solemn and ceremonious round dance, which is an essential part of every traditional festival or party.

Although anyone can join in the circle of the Sardana, another Catalan specialty, the *Castellers*, requires practice and some acrobatic talent. It encompasses a multistoried human pyramid, with strong men forming the base and often children climbing up to its peak. Six to nine (or so the record goes) stories can be built up in this way, cheered on by the masses. Valls in the Catalonian hinterland of the Costa Dorada is said to be the home of this dance, which has long since spread throughout the rest of Catalonia and time and again symbolizes the solidarity, stability and courage of the Catalan people.

San Jordi (St. George), the patron saint of Catalonia, is celebrated on every 23rd April. Part of this festival is swinging the Catalan flag fiercely at the central government in Madrid. Another festival falls on this day, which makes the celebration doubly worthwhile: it is in honor of Cervantes, the celebrated Catalan national writer. The anniversary of his death was declared *Book Day,* on which every lady bequeaths a book to her partner, father, brother or boss and he returns the favor by presenting her with a rose. The actual *National Day,* 11th September, is more like a day of mourning. The fact that the Bourbons, the victors of the War of Succession against the Habsburgs, annulled Catalonia's independence on this day in 1714, is held in remembrance.

The feast day of patron saints, *La Mercè* on 24th September, is a celebration which stretches over a five-day period in Barcelona and, at the same time, the summertime is also bade farewell. This is when the Catalans really show that they are not children of sadness. This festival has only been celebrated for the last 20 years, although it does incorporate many traditional elements. *Gegants*, giant figures made of papier-maché, sway through the streets. The ritual of the dancing giants dates back to the 14th century and is as popular as ever. It isn't only children who whoop with joy when the men beneath the huge dolls, encumbered by limited vision and the heavy weight on their shoulders, attempt quick dance steps. These giants are often accompanied by the *Correfoc,* which literally means wildfire. Devils and firework-spewing dragons parade through the crowds. Actors and spectators accompany the inferno with a dreadful racket, until San Jordi the Dragonslayer turns up and sets the world right again. The best Castellers groups in all of Catalonia are simply obliged to be present at this important celebration. They meet to compete against each other at the town hall square. On other squares throughout the city, the best bands give their all – from *Havaneres*, the melancholy song of seafarers setting sail for Cuba, to jazz and techno anthems. People dance and drink and everyone appearsa to be under the impression that the entire city of Barcelona has gathered for one huge family festival.

One further "fiery" festival is celebrated on the night from 23rd to 24th June. On the *Nit de Sant Joan*, or night of St. John, the summer solstice is celebrated. Music fills the streets while mountains of bulky household rubbish rise ever-higher on the roadsides, which are set alight after dark. And while the fires still crackle, rockets explode at midnight and the kind of fireworks which are only ever experienced on New Years Eve in other places dramatically light up the heavens here.

The traditional festival of fools, the *Carnival*, was strictly prohibited during the Franco era because the dictator feared that the Catalans might revolt in the midst of the masked hubbub. The carnival parade of Platja d'Aro on the Costa Brava has developed into the third-largest in Spain. A specialty amongst parades is, however, the transvestite carnival in Sitges, where the atmosphere and costumes are about as frivolous as they can possibly get.

And where would a wine-growing region be without its *wine festivals*. The small but outward-looking Sitges also leads the way in this department. On the third Sunday of every September, when the harvesting has already commenced inland, the wine queen is chosen. But the highlight of this festival is the wine crushers' competition. The juice is pounded from the grapes with all the strength the contestants can muster. The red juice squirts into the masses, who yell with all of their might for a rich harvest.

Festivals

Excellent Catalonian Cuisine

The landscape of northern Catalonia presents itself as wild and untamed between rugged bays and mountain peaks. The Catalans themselves are similar and are considered proud and independent, so it isn't surprising that many of their culinary creations have an element of daring about them.

When it comes to choosing ingredients, cooks in Catalonia are spoilt for choice. The Greeks and Romans brought the olive tree, the vine and wheat into the land and the salting of fish became a business staple in quite a few Costa Bravan towns, of which the famous *Anxoves* (anchovis) from L'Escala are evidence. The Moors also brought many types of fruit and vegetable into Spain. For as long as can be remembered, the Pyrenees have provided meats such as rabbit, lamb, par-

Above: Spicy ham (jamón) for starters. Right: Fish and seafood in the Boquería of Barcelona.

tridge, pork, game and goat. Herbs and mushrooms essential for many dishes, including the reddish-brown *Rovelló*, at which mushroom enthusiasts break into ecstasy, all flourish in the highlands. In the winter months, gourmets float on a cloud nine of truffels.

To transform the very best ingredients into memorable dishes, a wealth of fantasy and perhaps a pinch of madness is required. After all, how else could one possibly come up with the idea of combining chicken and lobster (*Pollastre amb llangosta*) on one plate and then adding the finishing touch of decorating this compound with chestnuts and truffels, or combining pig's knuckle with eggs and sugar *(Peuada)*, or dousing rabbit with chocolate sauce (*Conill a l'Empordanesa*).

Old Empordà, the region around Figueres which produced the fantastically-creative Dalí – albeit in an entirely different field, is considered a gourmet mecca. No wonder, one might think whilst perusing the menus which sometimes give the impression that the great surrealist master must surely have played a role himself in the composition of these concoctions. The manner of these extraordinary mixtures awakens astonishment and delights not only laypeople but also culinary professionals such as restaurant testers, who often cause showers of "stars" to fall on the best restaurants in this region.

The *entremeses* (starters) cunningly get you tuned-in to the main course. One is willingly served a colorful plate of various sausage types, but with a healthy addition of lots of vegetables. *Escalivada,* grilled vegetables in an olive oil paste, is an intrinsic part of every starter. *Esqueixada,* a delicious salad, combines fresh vegetables with dried cod (*bacallà*).

Rice and pasta dishes appear on every menu. The rice has always been grown in the Ebro delta of southern Costa Dorada and the rice dish *paella*, which originated

in Valencia, is by now a common term for every visitor to Spain. *Arròs negre,* a culinary highlight, might visually take a little getting used to though. Its mysterious color comes from squid ink.

Catalonia's penchant for pasta dishes, surprisingly not shared in the rest of Spain, stems from the Middle Ages when several Italian provinces belonged to the great maritime empire. *Fideus à la Catalana* is a variation on paella made of vermicelli, vegetables, fish and meat.

There is no shortage of meat in the mountainous, forested region of Catalonia and traditional cuisine preferred dishes to be solid. Wild boar is roasted together with chestnuts. Pork sausage (*botifarras*), high in fat, simply cannot be avoided and they can even be found swimming in Catalonia's favorite stew (*Escudella i carn d'olla*) together with chick peas, cabbage and various types of meat.

And seafood doesn't just turn out well when cooked in the pan. *Suquet de peix* is the name of a fish stew, rich in its variety of seafood. Especially fine species of fish still splash happily around the rocky bays of northern Catalonia, such as gurnard or red scorpion fish. In Roses, Palamós and Cambrils you should not miss out on the gambas, and anchovis from L'Escala have always been popular. Further inland trout is eaten, which – giving away its Arabian legacy – is served with almonds, figs and raisins.

The Catalans share their affinity for sauces of all types with their French neighbors: *Allioli,* a blend of garlic and olive oil accompanies most grilled dishes. *Picada* is bread roasted with almonds, garlic and parsley. *Romesco* extends the existing ingredients of Picada with the addition of tomatoes and peppers and adds that certain something to seafood dishes, whether it is served warm or cold. *Sofregit* consists of tomatoes steamed in oil, onions and garlic; the same sauce is known as *Samfaina* when puréed together with eggplant.

The Catalan weakness for all things sweet has influenced many a main

81

course. But there's no shortage of traditional sweets (*Postres*) either. The sweet-toothed simply rave for *Crema Catalana,* the national dessert, topped off with a hood of roasted sugar. Delicious baked specialties, but also tender, mellow cream cheese with honey (*Mel i Mató*), round off the dessert buffet.

So that the sumptuous food goes down more easily, Catalan wine-growers have created exceptional wines. Some of the vine-growing areas have won international acclaim in recent years. Among these are D.O. (registered mark of origin: *Denominació d'Origen*) Empordà-Costa Brava, D. O. Priorat, D. O. Tarragona, D. O. Terra Alta and above all D. O. Penedès with its astonishing variety, from light, fruity whites to aromatic reds, and not forgetting the famous sparkling *Cava* wines.

Catalan National Beverage

The sparkling wine flows furiously, the fact that evening has fallen is being celebrated once more. Joan pours another glass of delicious *Brut* – the establishment's own brand of course. In the Bar **Can Paixano**, in the middle of Barcelona's former fishing quarter of Ribera, locals as well as visitors desperately attempt to obtain one of the seats at the narrow, busy bar, to let a glass of *Cava* "sparkle" on their tongue. The solid tapas which Joan slides over the bar provide the stomach with adequate lining, and he sells the sparkling wet stuff at truly friendly prices. No wonder then, that it gets ordered by the bottle.

Catalan sparkling wine is becoming something of a cult experience, even beyond its own home. Since Spain joined the EU in 1986, Cavas have seduced their way into and are conquering the shelves of many a European supermarket.

Right: The renowned Cavas del Castillo de Perelada near Figueres.

The word has long since spread that these superb products from Catalan cava producers can easily hold their own with the more prestige-laden competition from the French Champagne region, but are considerably more inexpensive.

To trace the roots of this beverage one must go to Sadurni d'Anoia. The small town 40 kilometers southwest of Barcelona nestles in the Penedès, one of the most traditionally-wealthy wine-growing regions in Catalonia, and survives solely from the production of cava.

The first vines were introduced by early settlers, Greeks and Romans, from across the sea. The large monasteries of the region continued their viniculture throughout the Middle Ages and, little by little, improved the quality of their grape juice. Apart from the favorable climatic conditions, it was the Catalans' spirit for innovation and discovery which ensured that their simple table wines would soon have top-class, competitive counterparts. This, the middle of an old scape of vineyards, is where the history of Spanish sparkling wine began, and about 95% of the entire cava output is manufactured in Sant Sadurni and its surroundings.

A wine cellar visit should be the center of every trip into the wine region, but you'll be spoilt for choice: more than 100 cava cellars compete for popularity. A visit to the Pope of Cava at **Can Codorníu** is an absolute, unavoidable must.

Cava's hour of birth struck in 1872, when wine-grower Josep Raventós, who was married to Anna Codorníu of the successful wine-growing family with roots dating back to 1551, returned home from an educational trip to France. He had grown to know and love champagne there and began to copy the *méthode champenoise* with the grapes at home, which was based on the concept of bottle fermentation and dated back to the 17th century when famous monk Dom Perignon first tested the method.

The result was more than palatable and transpired just in time to christen Catalonia's rise to an industrial nation. *Xampán* was the name initially used for the drink, which naturally caused great consternation among the French. Following Spain's entry into the EU it was forced, due to pressure exerted by its neighbor, to find a new name for its beverage. At first *Cava* was only a compromise solution, which eventually became the permanent solution as *caves* quite simply means *(wine) cellars*.

Following its first fermentation the wine is filled into bottles, where it ripens for a minimum of nine months. Finer qualities of Cava ripen for longer. A second fermentation takes place within the bottle. It is necessary to shake the bottles so that the fermentation yeast settles on the corks and in the larger modern cellars this task is of course carried out by machinery, as about 40 million bottles of Cava are produced annually.

The oldest part of the time-honored winery of **Can Codorniu**, the holy halls, so to speak, were built toward the end of the 19th century by none other than Josep Puig i Cadafalch, one of the great maestros of *modernism,* or Catalan Art Nouveau. The tunnels leading into the chalk cliffs below the vineyards are impressive because of their breathtaking dimensions – about 100 million bottles of cava are stored in 5 storeys, each measuring 25 kilometers in length. The driest types of Cava – *Brut* and *Brut Natural*, remain in the country, whereas *Sec* and *Demi sec*, the sugar contents of which are considerably higher, are usually exported.

But the ultimate highlight of this tour is undoubtedly the "Temple of Cava", where the very first vine which produced the very first Cava has been bathed in bronze and decorated with colored baubles, just like a Christmas tree, and is worshipped like a holy relic. After such a sobering and noble encounter a glass of fine cava will help you wash down the lump in your throat and feel genuine gratitude toward the inventor of such a precious drink.

METRIC CONVERSION

Metric Unit	US Equivalent
Meter (m)	39.37 in.
Kilometer (km)	0.6241 mi.
Square Meter (sq m)	10.76 sq. ft.
Hectare (ha)	2.471 acres
Square Kilometer (sq km)	0.386 sq. mi.
Kilogram (kg)	2.2 lbs.
Liter (l)	1.05 qt.

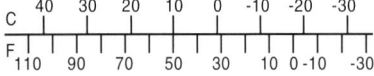

TRAVEL PREPARATIONS

Climate / Travel Season

The climate on the Costa Brava and Costa Dorada is Mediterranean, and in these areas it is accordingly windier, wetter and more changeable than in the sometimes very dry inland. Those holidaymakers interested mainly in a seaside holiday should visit the area in July/August, when summer weather can be guaranteed. Climatically pleasant months for more active outdoor holidays, as well as city breaks in Barcelona, are generally May, June and September. Most of the precipitation along these coastlines occurs between the months of March and May as well as between October and December.

On average the sun shines 200 days in the year and temperatures rarely exceed 35 ° C.

Healthcare

European holiday healthcare certificates are only valid for treatment in one of the state healthcare centers. Private health insurance for your holiday, which should also cover any family members traveling with you, is therefore highly recommended. Rates are generally quite acceptable. Doctors' fees are paid there and then and upon your return you can claim back these costs from your insurer.

You can inquire about English-speaking doctors at your hotel reception desk or at your consulate in Barcelona (addresses on p. 90).

Well-stocked pharmacies (*farmácias*) can be found in even the smallest town. A lot of medicines are sold without the necessity of a prescription. Opening times for pharmacies are the same as for shops. There is an emergency medical service, details of which are displayed on the door of every farmácia.

Entry Requirements / Visas

Spain has no visa regulations, but may soon introduce them for some African countries.

All that you will need to enter the country is a valid passport. Members of the European Community can enter with their national identity card.

Customs and Import Regulations

For private travel and personal use within the EU most goods are not restricted. The following are restricted and only the given amounts may be brought from other EU countries into Spain: 800 cigarettes, 400 cigarillos or 200 cigars, 1 kilogram of tobacco, 10 liters of spirits, 20 liters of other alcoholic drinks (max. 22% alcohol content), 90 liters of wine (max. 60 liters of sparkling wine), 110 liters of beer.

People entering Spain from non-EU countries may bring up to 10 kilograms of food and non-alcoholic drinks, 200 cigarettes or 250 grams of tobacco, and 1 liter of spirits or 2 liters of wine.

The same limits apply to all goods bought from duty-free shops (airports, ferries) in a non-EU country before arrival in Spain, as well as from duty-free shops in Spain before arrival in a non-EU country. Duty-free shopping on journeys between EU countries has been abolished since 1999.

There are no restrictions on bank checks and travelers checks in foreign currencies, as well as pesetas or other foreign currencies in the form of bank notes.

Currency / Foreign Exchange / Banks

The currency of Spain is the peseta (EPS). Notes circulate in denominations of 10,000, 5,000, 2,000 and 1,000 and coins in denominations of 500, 200, 100, 50, 25, 10, 5 and 1 peseta.

Rates of Exchange (at time of printing): 1 Euro = 166 EPS; 1 US Dollar = 199 EPS; 1 GB Pound = 285 EPS.

Cash-dispensers (*telebancos*) are everywhere and cash can be withdrawn with Eurocheque and Visa cards and most credit cards, so the dispensers tend to make a trip into the bank superfluous.

But should the machine be out of order, you may withdraw up to a maximum of 25,000 EPS by cashing in a Eurocheque at the counter. Identification will be necessary.

Bank opening hours: Mon-Fri 9 am-2 pm, some banks also open Saturdays from 9 am-12:30 pm. The bureaux de change in the tourist centers have longer opening hours but charge higher fees. Furthermore, money exchange in most of the larger hotels is usually not at a favorable rate.

GETTING THERE

By Plane

The most convenient way to get to Spain is by plane (terminals A and B service international flights). Flying is highly recommended for city breaks, as it is hard to find somewhere to park in most towns. Once you get there you can hire a car for excursions.

Most international airlines service Barcelona and all major car rental companies are represented there. There is also a bus service which takes you the 13 kilometers from the airport into the city and back. Buses run 7 days a week from about 6 am until about midnight, every 15 minutes. Journey time is approx. 40 minutes.

By Car

If you arrive by car you can travel from the British Isles by ferry and drive through France or northern Spain. The quickest routes from Europe are the coastal motorways (e.g. the A7 from France to Catalonia's coasts) which go around the Pyrenees. But the Pyrenees can be easily crossed in one day, either by using one of the passes or the Viella tunnel.

By Bus

All major international bus operators organize trips to Barcelona from most European cities and also from England. Be prepared for a long journey but there may be some great sightseeing along the way. Information at your nearest tour operator.

By Train

Barcelona is networked with all major European cities.

TRAVELING IN SPAIN

By Car

Both the A 7 and A 19 *autopistas* (highways) are toll roads but due to this fact they are rarely as overcrowded as the toll-free roads.

Speed limits: 90 km/h on secondary roads, 50 km/h in built-up areas, 100 km/h on major cross-country roads (at least 3 lanes) and 120 km/h on autopistas. 70 km/h or 80 km/h on the autopistas for cars with a trailer. Exceeding the speed limit will earn you a severe penalty.

Rules to remember: 1) No overtaking 100 meters before a hill as well as on roads where the view ahead is less than 200 meters. 2) Towing between private vehicles is prohibited. 3) Car phones are only permitted if used in combination with a hands-free unit.

The alcohol limit for drivers is 0.5 ‰.

Traffic signs: *Alto* = stop; *Atencion, Ciudado* = attention, beware; *Viraje* *peligroso* = dangerous bend; *Ceda al Paso* = give way; *Paso prohibido* = no through road; *Prohibido aparcar* = parking prohibited.

Accident / breakdown: The Reial Automobil Club de Catalunya is affiliated with some major motoring clubs but there is a national emergency breakdown service available round the clock, tel. 915 933333.

The police should be informed immediately (092) if an accident has occurred. Furthermore, international accident insurance, which is available from your own insurer, accident and repair cover from your automobile club and a motoring legal costs insurance are well worth taking out for the duration of your holiday.

Parking: As it's relatively difficult to find parking spaces in cities, it is highly recommendable to follow official parking directions. As well as in the usual supervised car parks, parking is also permitted in zones where the curb is marked blue, and these spaces are subject to a fee (ticket). In yellow zones parking is not permitted at all. Traffic wardens and towing services (GRUA) make no exceptions for offences caused by tourists.

Rental cars: Local companies often have better rates than the larger national and international rental firms (for example those in Barcelona and at the airports). The bill is paid in advance. If you don't have a credit card with you then as a rule you will have to leave a considerable deposit. It is advisable to take out comprehensive and passenger insurance when renting motor vehicles.

By Bus

Public transportation in Catalonia is mainly carried out by buses which also service small villages, but often only once a day. Information is available at hotel reception desks and from bus companies. The *Sarfa* bus company (tel: 932 651158) offers the best connections between Barcelona and the towns of the Costa Brava.

By Train

Besides the RENFE state trains, 27 *Ferrocarrils de la Generalitat* (an autonomous Catalan rail company) trains run back and forth on the Barcelona-Girona and Girona-Portbou routes. The Barcelona-Tarragona-Tortosa and Barcelona-Tarragona-Lleida routes are the most important in the Costa Dorada region.

PRACTICAL TIPS FROM A TO Z

Accommodation

An advance reservation for a visit planned in high season is absolutely essential. During this time, prices are at their peak. Low season prices are much cheaper.

Paradores: These state-owned hotels usually have an exclusive and interesting atmosphere. They were partly established in historical buildings and offer a standard of at least 3 or 4-star comfort. The only Parador on the Catalan coast is on the Costa Brava (**Parador de Turismo Aiguablava**, tel: 972 622162). A historic Parador has been established in the old castle of Tortosa on the southern Costa Dorada (**Parador de la Zuda**, Tortosa, tel: 977 444450).

Hotels: Spanish hotels (H) are classified on a scale of 1 to 5 stars according to their comfort and facilities. In S'Agaro on the Costa Brava the **Hostal de la Gavina** is one of a total of six establishments in all of Spain which are in a class of their own: GL or *Gran Lujo* (grand luxury).

Hostels / guest houses / rooms:
These are classified into three categories. Depending upon comfort, location and price (although depending on the season the prices of accommodation can vary greatly within the same category). Signs with the message *Camas* (beds) or

Habitaciones (rooms) imply private accommodation.

Hotels and other accommodation quoted in the guideposts are marked according to their price class:

☺ Double-rooms up to 8,000 pesetas

☺☺ Double-rooms between 8,000 and 16,000 pesetas

☺☺☺ Double-rooms from 16,000 pesetas.

Holiday apartments and houses:
These are best booked through a travel agent. The extensive variety ranges from apartments in anonymous high-rises located in large resorts to idyllic summer houses off the coast.

Holiday houses and smaller hotels can be booked at: www.terraviva.com

Youth hostels *(Albergues Juveniles):* Your international youth hostel identification will be necessary. Barcelona's youth hostel is located in the Sant Martí quarter: **Hostal de Joves de la Ciutadella**, Passeig Pujades 29, tel: 933 003104.

Camp sites: There are more than 300 camp sites along the Costa Brava. They all differ in convenience of location and amenities. Both of these factors influence price. Most sites are open from May through October, but a stay during the high season should definitely be booked in advance.

Eating and Drinking

Mealtimes and eating habits are very different to those of central Europe. Breakfast (*esmorcar*) is generally ignored and instead one grabs a coffee and croissant in a café or bar on the way to work. Lunch is eaten late, around 2 or 3 pm, like dinner which isn't normally served until about 10 pm. A traditional Catalan restaurant will hardly be open before 9 pm. But most tourist resorts and hotels have adapted to middle and northern European mealtimes. Many restaurants offer a good-value menu (*menú del día*) at midday.

Hunger between meals can be satisfied with small tapas and appetizers in the bars.

Here, wine and (still) mineral water accompany every meal and the youth tends to opt for beer more and more. *Cava* makes for a wonderful aperitif which sometimes also accompanies the meal (see feature p. 82).

Three of the most popular coffee varieties in Spain are: *cafè solo* (espresso), cortat/ *cortado* (espresso with milk) or *cafè am llet/* café con leche (café latte/au lait).

Restaurants: One waits in the restaurant until one is directed to a table. It is unthinkable to sit onesself down at a table with other guests, even if the restaurant is full.

Separate bills from the same table are unheard of in Spain. Either one party pays for all or the bill is divided into equal portions. But some of the tourist establishments have grundgingly adapted to these central European customs.

Holidays / Festivals / Events
Public holidays:
1st January: *Any Nou* (New Year); 6th January: *Reis Mags* (Epiphany)
19th March: *Sant Josep* (St. Joseph's Day); March/April: Good Friday and Easter
1st May: *Diada del Traball* (Day of Work)
29th June: *Sant Pere i San Pau* (Peter and Paul)
25th July: *Sant Jaume* (St. Jakob's Day)
15th August: *Assumpció* (Assumption)
11th September: *La Diada* (Catalan National Day); 24th September: *La Mercé* (Day of the Holy Virgin)
12th October: *Diada de la Hispanitat* (America Day, Spanish National Day)
1st November: *Tots Sants* (All Saints)
6th December: *Dia de la Constitució* (Constitution Day); 8th December: *Immaculat Concepció* (Immaculate Conception)

25th December: *Nadal* (Christmas); 26th December: *Sant Esteve* (St. Stephen's Day)

Festivals brighten up everyday life in Catalonia, although most are determined by the Catholic church's festival calendar. Here are a few of the most interesting festivals for tourists. More information is available at the tourist offices (see also "Festivals" on p. 78):

February: Transvestite Carnival in Sitges.

March/April: Holy Week celebrations in all of Spain, particularly in Girona in Catalonia; 23rd April: Double festival in all of Catalonia – celebration of Catalan patron saint San Jordi (St. George) and also the annual celebration of Book Day (anniversary of the death of Spanish writer Cervantes).

June: Corpus Christ parades, Summer Solstice (*Nit de Sant Joan*) and Feast of St. John on 23rd/24th June.

July: Sea processions in honor of the *Verge del Carmen* in Palamós; *Habaneras* festival in Calella de Palafrugell; Firework competitions in Blanes.

24th August: Patron saint festival in Lloret de Mar with large procession in honor of St. Cristina.

September: *Festa Major de la Mercé* – four-day celebrations also with music events and fire-walking in remembrance of the patron saint of Barcelona; Wine festivals in Llança and Sitges (3rd Sunday in September); 23rd September: Feast of patron St. Thekla in Tarragona.

October: **Sea Day** in Sant Feliú de Guixols.

December: *Festa de Santa Llúcia* in L'Estartit.

Cultural events:

April-June: Festival of antique, religious and romantic music by the "La Caixa" foundation in Barcelona.

June-August: El-Greco summer festival with theater, music, opera and dance in the Greek theater at Montjuic (Barcelona).

July/August: International music festival in Sant Feliú de Guixols.

September/October: Barcelona's International Film Festival and the International Jazz Festival in the city's Palau de la Musica. Festival of the Fantastic Film in Sitges.

October: Opening of the opera season in the Gran Teatre de Liceu in Barcelona.

Newspapers / Press

In Barcelona and the larger resorts a wide selection of foreign newspapers is available.

Post

Stamps (*sellos*) are available in post offices (*correos*) and tobacconists (*estanc/estanco*). Postcards and letters up to 20 g cost about 70 pesetas. Generally you can only phone from post offices, not fax.

Post Office opening hours: Mon-Fri 9 am-1 pm and 4-6 pm, Sat 9 am-1 pm.

Shopping

Barcelona offers an overwhelming, although not cheap, variety of shopping possibilities. Clothes are definitely a recommendable bargain, for example in the many inexpensive chain stores such as *Zara* and *Mango*. Shoes are often also a bargain.

Visiting the **markets** is well worthwhile. Most coastal towns have a once-weekly market: Monday (Blanes, Cadaqués, Torroella de Montgri), Tuesday (Lloret de Mar, Palamós), Wednesday (Llança), Thursday (L'Estartit, Tossa de Mar), Friday (Platja d'Aro, Port de la Selva), Saturday (Girona), Sunday (L'Escala, Roses, Sant Feliú de Guixols).

Opening hours: 9:30 am-1:30 pm (or 10 am-2 pm) and 6-7:30 pm (or 4:30-8 pm).

Opening hours are not governed by law in Spain and can vary depending on the season and the establishment. Department stores are generally open from 10 am to 9 pm, many of them on Sundays also but for a shorter time.

Sports

Golf: Golfers will be thrilled at the numerous, beautifully-situated, mostly 18-hole courses. A list of all the courses along the coast and further detailed information is available from the Federació Catalana de Golf, C/ Aribau 382, 08006 Barcelona, tel. 934 145262, fax 934 584102.

Horseback Riding: Information on riding in the Costa Brava region – inland or coasts – is available from the Catalan Riders Association, tel: 972 204650.

Hiking: The northern Costa Brava is particularly satisfying terrain for hikers. Hikes can be made along the rocky coastline, and excursions into the Pyrenees are very charming. Hiking boots are a must. Hiking maps (which aren't always up to date) can be purchased in the bookshops of every town.

Water sports: Above all it's the northern part of Costa Brava which has proven itself a windsurfers' mecca, while the rocky stretches of coast around the Illes Medes by l'Estartit provide some fantastic diving and snorkeling. Sailors will find the best conditions around Palamós, Platja d'Aro and Roses. Detailed information on harbors are available from the Associació Catalana de Ports Esportius i Turistics, C/ Provenca 385, 08025 Barcelona, tel: 934 584101.

Furthermore, tourist offices provide information on every type of sport. Interesting and informative material on "active tourism" is available from: Department d'Industria, Comerç i Turisme de la Generalitat de Catalunya, Passeig de Gracia 105, 08008 Barcelona, tel: 934 849900, fax: 934 849888.

Taxis

Taxis are a relatively cheap method of transportation in Spain and they are always equipped with meters. Taxi stands are always plentiful, but taxis can also be waved down. It is normal to give drivers a small tip.

Telecommunications

Provincial area codes in Spain have been an intrinsic part of telephone numbers for several years, which means that they must also always be dialled for local calls.

Spain's country code is +34 ("+" usually denoting "00". Some national codes from Spain are as follows: England +44, Switzerland +41, France +33, Canada and USA +1, Holland +31, Ireland +353, New Zealand +64, Australia +61). If you then dial the area code the first "0" must be omitted.

Calls from public telephone boxes can be made with either coins or with phone cards, all from the same box. Phone cards are available in tobacconists and in some souvenir shops.

In Barcelona there are several internet cafés, as well as in Girona, Tarragona and several other resort towns.

Theft

Petty crime is unfortunately very common in Spain. You can avoid it by depositing valuables in your hotel safe or at least in a locked suitcase and by not carrying more cash than necessary. Ladies should keep an eye on their bags and any wallets are best kept in front, not back, pockets.

Do not leave any belongings such as jackets, blankets etc., in your car. Car radios also attract thieves.

Any theft must be reported to the police immediately in order to claim back any insurance for stolen items upon your return home. If your passport has been stolen, you will need to contact your country's embassy in Barcelona.

Timezone

All of Spain (with the exception of the Canary Islands in the Atlantic) belongs to

Travel Information

the Central European Time zone (CET). Clocks are changed over to summer time (for seven months) on the last weekend in March.

Tipping
Tips are already included in all restaurant prices, but an additional tip of between 5 and 10 % of the total bill is usually expected. A tip is not normally given until the remaining change has been handed over to the guest, who should then leave the tip on a plate on the table or at the bar.

It is also common to give small tips to porters, hotel staff and taxi drivers.

Tourist Information
Tourist information offices (*Oficina de Turisme*) are generally found everywhere, even in smaller towns, where many of them are part of the local town hall (*Ajuntament*) (for addresses see guideposts at the end of each chapter). Their informative material (town maps, hotel index and events calendars) is very helpful and available in English. Opening hours are as for shops, but in larger tourist areas they are also open on Sunday mornings in the summertime.

Barcelona's international airport, Prat de Llobregat, has information on all the regions of Spain, tel: 934 784704.

ADDRESSES

Catalan Tourism Department:
Centre d'Informació Turística de Catalunya, Palau Robert, Passeig de Gràcia 107, 08008 Barcelona, tel: 932 384000, fax 932 384010.
Concordi de Promoció Turística de Catalunya, Generalitat de Catalunya, Passeig Gracià 112, 08008 Barcelona, tel: 932 176979, fax 934 151434.

Diplomatic Representation:
American Consulate: Reina Elisenda 23, 08034 Barcelona, tel: 932 802227.

British Consulate: Av. Diagonale 477, 13th floor, 08036 Torre de Barcelona, tel: 933 666200.
Canadian Embassy (Madrid only): Nuñes de Balboa 35, Madrid, tel: 914 233250.
Consulate of Ireland: Gran Via Carles III 94, 08028 Barcelona. Tel. 934 915021.

USEFUL WEBSITES
www.barcelona.de
www.cbrava.es
www.publintur.es
www.tourism.catalonia.net

LANGUAGE GUIDE

General

English	Spanish	Catalan
Good morning/day	Buenos días	Bon dia
Good day (after midday)	Buenas tardes	Bona tarde
Good night	Buenas noches	Bona nit
Hello (to friends)	¡Hola!	Hola!
Bye	Adiós	Adéu
See you later	Hasta luego	Fins després
How are you?	¿Cómo esta?	Com va?
Very well, thank you!	Muy bien, gracias	Molt bé, gràcies
Please (request)	Por favor	Si us plau
Excuse me	Perdón	Perdó
I'm sorryLo siento		Ho sento
Thank you very much	Muchas gracias	Moltes gràcies
Yes/no	Si/No	Si/No
Do you speak English?	¿Habla Usted inglés?/	Parla anglès?
I don't understand Spanish	No entiendo español	No entenc espanyol
A little slower please	Mas lento, por favor	Més a poc a poc, per favor
What is your name?	¿Cómo se llama Usted?	Com et dius?
My name is ...	Me llamo ...	Em dic ...
How do I get to ...?	¿Cómo llego a ...?	Com puc anar a...?
Where can I get ...?	¿Donde hay ...?	On puc trobar ...?
Where are the toilets?	¿Donde hay los servicios?	On són es serveis?
Who/when/where to/what?	¿Quien/Cuando/Adonde/Qué?	Qui/Quan/A on/Què?
What's the price of ...?	¿Cuanto cuesta ...?	Quant val ...?
That is too expensive	E demasiado caro	Es massa car
How far is it to ...?	¿Cuantos kilómetros son hasta ...?	Com és de lluny ...?
What time is it?	¿Qué hora es?	Quina hora és?
Yesterday/today/tomorrow	ayer/hoy/mañana	ahir/avui/demà
Very good/bad	muy bien/mal	molt bo/mal
Expensive/cheapæ	caro/barrato	car(a)/barat(a)

Accommodation

Do you have a room free	¿Tiene Usted una habitación libre	Té una habitació iliure?
Double/single roooom	Habitación doble/individual	Habitació doble individual
Can I see the room	¿Puedo ver la habitación?	Puc veure l'habitació?
Hotel/guesthouse	Hotel/Pensión	Hotel/Pensió
For one night/week	Para una noche/semana	Per una nit/una setmana

Numbers

0/1/2	cero/un(o)/dos	zero/u (un, una)/dues
3/4/5	tres/cuatro/cinco	tres/quatre/cinc

Travel Information

91

6/7/8 . . . . *seis/siete/ocho*. . . . . sis/set/vuit
9/10/11/12 . . . . *nueve/diez/once/doce* . . . . . nou/deu/onze/dotze
20/50/100 . . . . *veinte/cincuenta/cien(to)* . . . vint/cinquanta/cien
1000/10 000 . . . . . . *mil/diez mil* . . . . mil/deu mil

Traveling

I'd like a car (to rent) . . . *Quisiera alquilar un coche* . . Voldria llogar un cotxe
To the left/right . . . . . . *A la izquierda/derecha* . . . . a l'esquerra/a la dreta
Straight ahead. . . . . . . *Siempre derecho* . . . . tot dret
Above/below . . . . *arriba/abajo* . . . . dalt/a baix
Street/freeway . . . . . *Calle/Carretera* . . . . Carrer/Carretera
Avenue . . . . *Avenida* . . . . Avinguda
Tourist information . . . . *Información turística* . . . . . Informació turística
Airport/airplane. . . . . . *aeroperto/avión/vuelo*. . . . . aeroport/avió/vol
Car/taxi . . . . *coche/taxi* . . . . cotxe/taxi
Train/station/platform . . *tren/estación/andén* . . . . . tren/estació/andana
Boat/harbor. . . . . *barco/puerto* . . . . vaixell/port
Ticket . . . . *billete* . . . . bitllet
There (and back) . . . . *ida (y vuelta)* . . . . anada (i tornada)
Open/closed. . . . . . . *abierto / cerrado* . . . . . . obert/tancat
Post office/stamp . . . . *Correos/sello* . . . . Correus/segell
Address/telephone . . . . *dirección/teléfono*. . . . . . adreça/telèfon

In the restaurant

The menu, please! . . . . *¡La lista de platos/* . . . . . La carta, si us plau!
                                 del menú, por favor!
The bill, please!   *¡La cuenta, por favor!*   Es compte, si us plau!
Bon appetit!. . . . . . . *¡Que aproveche!* . . . . Bon profit!
Starter/soup . . . . *entremeses/sopas* . . . . . . entremès/sopa
Dessert/fish . . . . *postres/pescado* . . . . postres/peix
Mussels . . . . *mejillones* . . . . musclos
Tintenfischringe . . . . . *calamares* . . . . calamars
Crab/lobster. . . . . . . *gambas/langosta* . . . . . . gambes/llagosta
Tuna/perch . . . . *atún/mero* . . . . tonyina/mero
Meat/poultry . . . . *carne/aves*. . . . . carn/ars
Beef/pork . . . . *carne de vaca/cerdo* . . . . . carn de vaca/porc
Mutton/chicken. . . . . . *cordero/pollo* . . . . xai/pollastre
Rabbit/suckling pig. . . . *conejo/conchinillo* . . . . . conill/porcelleta
Salad/vegetables . . . . *ensalada/verduras* . . . . . amanida/verdures
Fruit. . . . . *fruta*. . . . . fruita
Apple/orange . . . . . . *manzana/naranja* . . . . . . poma/taronja
Bread/cheese . . . . . . *pan/queso* . . . . pa/formatge
Ham/salami. . . . . . . *jamón/salchichón* . . . . . . pernil/salchichon
Lard biscuits . . . . . . *ensaimada*. . . . . ensaïmada
Pasta/rice . . . . *pastas/arroz*. . . . . pasta/arròs
Potatoes. . . . . *papas (patatas)* . . . . patates
Drinks/water . . . . . . *bebidas/agua* . . . . begudas/aigua
Red-/white wine . . . . *vino tinto/blanco* . . . . . . vi negre/blanc
Beer. . . . . *cerveza* . . . . cervesa

AUTHORS

Elke Homburg has studied literature, drama and philosophy, and has been traveling throughout Spain as a study-tour director for many years. As a freelance journalist and author she has had several of her books about the Iberian peninsula published.

Marion Golder works as a travel writer and director of study tours, mainly in Spain and Latin America. Spain has long since become her second home and she wrote the chapter on "Barcelona".

Both authors have also worked on the title *Andalusia*, also from this series.

PHOTOGRAPHERS

Amberg, Gunda   81
Art and history archives,
    Berlin   8, 9
Beck, Josef (Silvestris)   55
Cavas del Castillo del Perelada,
    Peralada, Spain   83
Drölle, Frank (PhotoPress)   16, 18
Durazzo, Michelangelo
    (Viesti Associates)   14
Fischer, Peter   cover, 15
Fritz, Wolfgang   29, 58/59, 80
Homburg, Elke   27, 34, 77
Kanzler, Thomas   22, 51
Liese, Knut   12, 19, 23, 30R, 33, 37,
                                       60, 65, 71, 78
Master (PhotoPress)   10/11
Paraíso Gonzales, Angeles   28
Prieto, José Ignacio   70
Schlierbach, Karl-Heinz
    (PhotoPress)   26
Scholten, Jo   74/75
Stadler, Otto (Silvestris)   3, 25, 31, 35,
                                     38, 39, 40, 41
Thiele, Klaus   68
Wenzel, Thomas (PhotoPress)   46

Travel Information

93

INDEX

94

Explore the World

AVAILABLE TITELS

Afghanistan 1 : 1 500 000
Argentina *(Northern),* **Uruguay**
 1 : 2 500 000
Argentina *(Southern),* **Uruguay**
 1 : 2 500 000
Australia 1 : 4 000 000
Bangkok - *and Greater Bangkok*
 1 : 75 000 / 1 : 15 000
Burma → *Myanmar*
Caribbean - **Bermuda, Bahamas,**
 Greater Antilles 1 : 2 500 000
Caribbean - **Lesser Antilles**
 1 : 2 500 000
Central America 1 : 1 750 000
Central Asia 1 : 1 750 000
Chile 1 : 2 500 000
China - *Northeastern*
 1 : 1 500 000
China - *Northern* 1 : 1 500 000
China - *Central* 1 : 1 500 000
China - *Southern* 1 : 1 500 000
Colombia - Ecuador 1 : 2 500 000
Crete - Kreta 1 : 200 000
Cuba 1 : 775 000
Dominican Republic - Haiti
 1 : 600 000
Egypt 1 : 2 500 000 / 1 : 750 000
Hawaiian Islands
 1 : 330 000 / 1 : 125 000

Hawaiian Islands – **Kaua'i**
 1 : 150 000 / 1 : 35 000
Hawaiian Islands – **Honolulu**
 - O'ahu 1 : 35 000 / 1 : 150 000
Hawaiian Islands – **Maui - Moloka'i**
 - Lāna'i 1 : 150 000 / 1 : 35 000
Hawaiian Islands – **Hawai'i, The Big**
 Island 1 : 330 000 / 1 : 125 000
Himalaya 1 : 1 500 000
Hong Kong 1 : 22 500
Indian Subcontinent 1 : 4 000 000
India - *Northern* 1 : 1 500 000
India - *Western* 1 : 1 500 000
India - *Eastern* 1 : 1 500 000
India - *Southern* 1 : 1 500 000
India - *Northeastern - Bangladesh*
 1 : 1 500 000
Indonesia 1 : 4 000 000
Indonesia **Sumatra** 1 : 1 500 000
Indonesia **Java - Nusa Tenggara**
 1 : 1 500 000
Indonesia **Bali - Lombok**
 1 : 180 000
Indonesia **Kalimantan**
 1 : 1 500 000
Indonesia **Java - Bali** 1 : 650 000
Indonesia **Sulawesi** 1 : 1 500 000
Indonesia **Irian Jaya - Maluku**
 1 : 1 500 000
Jakarta 1 : 22 500
Japan 1 : 1 500 000

Kenya 1 : 1 100 000
Korea 1 : 1 500 000
Malaysia 1 : 1 500 000
West Malaysia 1 : 650 000
Manila 1 : 17 500
Mexico 1 : 2 500 000
Myanmar (Burma) 1 : 1 500 000
Nepal 1 : 500 000 / 1 : 1 500 000
Nepal Trekking **Khumbu Himal -**
 Solu Khumbu 1 : 75 000
New Zealand 1 : 1 250 000
Pakistan 1 : 1 500 000
Peru - Ecuador 1 : 2 500 000
Philippines 1 : 1 500 000
Singapore 1 : 22 500
Southeast Asia 1 : 4 000 000
South Pacific Islands 1 : 13 000 000
Sri Lanka 1 : 450 000
Taiwan 1 : 400 000
Tanzania - Rwanda, Burundi
 1 : 1 500 000
Thailand 1 : 1 500 000
Uganda 1 : 700 000
Venezuela - Guyana, Suriname,
 French Guiana 1 : 2 500 000
Vietnam, Laos, Cambodia
 1 : 1 500 000

FORTHCOMING

Bolivia, Paraguay 1 : 2 500 000

Nelles Maps are top quality cartography!
Relief mapping, kilometer charts and tourist attractions.
Always up-to-date!